The ANATOMY OF COURAGE

The

ANATOMY
OF
COURAGE

LORD MORAN

AVERY PUBLISHING GROUP INC.

Garden City Park, New York

First published in 1945. Second edition issued 1966.
Avery's Art of Command series edition published 1987.

Reprinted through special arrangement with Constable & Company
Ltd., London.
ISBN 0-89529-283-1

Contents

Part three THE CARE AND MANAGEMENT OF FEAR

DEDICATED

to
MY FATHER
who was without fear
by
HIS SON
who is less fortunate

Acknowledgments

I want to thank: first Sir Winston Churchill who took me where I might learn from those who were doing the fighting: Group Captain Corner, who, until he was killed, acted as my pilot in more senses than one to units of the Fighter and Bomber commands; Lady Desborough, Mr. Desmond MacCarthy, Dr. H. K. Prescot and my wife for criticism and advice: and the officers and men of the First Battalion The Royal Fusiliers, who taught me what men can do in war.

Preface

to the second edition

In the summer of 1919, on my return from the war in France, I read in *The Times* that a Royal Commission on shell-shock had been set up, which did not contain among its members anyone who had been near the trenches. I decided to write to *The Times*. A friend pointed out that as I was quite unknown I should keep my letter short if I wanted to have it published. I felt too strongly to fall in with this advice, and my letter grew into a long essay on courage. When it was finished my wife took it down on a bicycle to Printing House Square. Days went by and nothing appeared and I assumed that my script had been rejected, when one day I found it on the middle page of *The Times*. It took up a whole column. So encouraged I sat down and wrote a second letter on the relations of Capital and Labour. My luck was in, and next day a column and a quarter of the middle page carried my message.

My two letters were read by Curtis Brown, a prominent literary agent, who asked me to call on him. He invited me to write a book based on my letters. I was excited, but when he began to question me how my days were spent he shook his head. "You cannot write while you are leading that kind of life," he grunted. He was right, and in fact it was twenty-five years before I found time to put together *The Anatomy of Courage*.

But from that day I began to gather material for the book. A young soldier, Goschen by name, read the letters and made up his mind that if ever he was given a position of responsibility, he would ask the writer to talk to his men on courage and fear. Fifteen years passed before he became Commandant of the Royal Military Academy at Woolwich. But he had not forgotten. One raw evening in November I found myself in a gymnasium full of fog, trying to decipher my notes by the dim light of a reading lamp.

Word went round and I was invited to address various Commands, and to meet some of the pilots in the Air Force. Group Captain Corner used to fly me in his two-seater Moth to the airfields until he was shot down. But I owe most to the Staff College at Camberley where I lectured on my subject for a number of years to very lively audiences. Quick to take my points they brought to the debate the harvest of years of experience in the handling of their men. I was pressed by those who came to these lectures to put something on paper, and this was how my book began.

It was not published until the turn of the year, 1944, the year of the invasion of Europe and the liberation of France. It is a study of men under the stress of war, based on diaries which I kept while serving in the trenches with the First Battalion of the Royal Fusiliers, from the Autumn 1914 to the Spring of 1917. It is but a step to my book on Sir Winston Churchill where I set out to describe the effect of strain on a single individual from the record in my diary of the twenty-five years during which I was associated with him.

My faith is that the martial spirit of a race is in a measure a crucial test of it's virility, and that a man of character in peace is a man of courage in war. Is it not true that the early discovery of fear is as important in one army as in another? And if I am right that the morale of all armies broke sooner or later then it is not in England only that we ought to enquire into our modern equipment for meeting great adventures.

10 June, 1966.

Preface

to the first edition

In this book I set out to find how courage is born and how
it is sustained in a modern army of a free people. The
soldier is alone in his war with terror and we have to recognise the first signs of his defeat that we may come in time
to his rescue. So the first part describes the discovery of
fear. The second tells how courage is spent in war. In the
third part of the book—The Care and Management of Fear
—I tell what can be done to delay or prevent this using up
of courage.

What was happening in men's minds? How were they
wearing? Those were the only questions that seemed to
matter during my years with a battalion in France. They
are of everlasting consequence in war. It was my business
as a doctor to find answers to such questions in time to rest
a soldier who was not wearing well, that he might once
more quit himself like a man.

In the chapters which I have called the Discovery of Fear
I have tried to show how this was done. If the doctor knew
his men he could often detect some change in their manner
or way of speech that warned him before it was too late.
The "Birth of Fear" is the record of my vigil with the First

Battalion of the Royal Fusiliers from the autumn of 1914 to the spring of 1917, to which I have added what I have learnt from pilots of the Air Force in this war. But to find fear in its infancy is not always so simple. There were sensitive men to whom the last war was purgatory, who yet contrived a mask of indifference so that they were accepted as imperturbable and were put in authority over others. When their self-control wore thin they were given to moods, which was the language in which they spoke to us of their distresses. To detect such moods and to recognise how they arose is an essential part of the early discovery of fear.

How is courage spent in war? Courage is will-power, whereof no man has an unlimited stock; and when in war it is used up, he is finished. A man's courage is his capital and he is always spending. The call on the bank may be only the daily drain of the front line or it may be a sudden draft which threatens to close the account. His will is perhaps almost destroyed by intensive shelling, by heavy bombing, or by a bloody battle, or it is gradually used up by monotony, by exposure, by the loss of the support of stauncher spirits on whom he has come to depend, by physical exhaustion, by a wrong attitude to danger, to casualties, to war, to death itself.

Mr. Duff Cooper, in his life of Lord Haig, has put forward another view of courage. He writes that the British went into the battle of the Somme a citizen army only half trained to war and that the survivors in mid-November were veterans. The British were taught to fight. While I affirm that men wear out in war like clothes. Are soldiers to be seasoned by constant fighting, or are they to be spared that they may last the longer? The issue is fundamental, it affects policy. I have therefore given my diary of the Somme that the reader may judge between us. In a battle the soldier's senses are dulled, but even if he comes out unscathed the ordeal may shorten his life in the line, while in a trench raid, which I have described to point the contrast, the raiders' faculties are on the alert but the effect is more fleeting, the scars are less deep.

In the "Care and Management of Fear" I start with selection, since if an army is being prepared to fight it ought to begin by eliminating those who are incapable of fighting. I pass to the need of a corporate opinion in a battalion, which shall build up standards of conduct. And as an illustration I have chosen the small army who laid down their arms in 1917 and 1918 because they had got it into their heads that they were gassed. Leadership only concerns me when it hastens or delays the using up of the soldier's will-power. But discipline runs through this part of my book like an undertone. Men are everywhere demanding whether a discipline which was designed for the illiterate is still suitable for an army with a considerable number of thinking men in its ranks. I have turned over in my mind whether it is possible to relax that discipline without impairing the soldier's efficiency as a fighting man, and I can find only one answer in the story of war. There is nothing in the life of our times to suggest that we can make an exception now with impunity. In a democracy we need more, not less, discipline, if by discipline we mean self control. And this need is underlined by the manner in which this generation in England was prepared in peace for the ordeal of battle. The fluid mind of youth has been baffled and confused by events which have mostly arisen out of the last war. Brought up at the feet of those who served in the citizen army of that war, they have been nurtured on tales of Passchendaele and the Somme, they are prepared for any story of ineptitude. They have been taught that war is a senseless folly which solves nothing. They are sceptical and critical.

While this was happening in England, the Germans were busy applying the lessons of the last war. One of the causes of their defeat, they asserted, was that the mind of their people, and in particular of their youth, had not been prepared in peace for the trials of war. They did not intend to repeat that mistake. There was a veritable toilet of the mind—even their school books were doctored—to inculcate into the whole German nation the prized qualities of the soldier. Happily no democracy can be prepared in the German sense for war—we are of course paying in full for this freedom of the mind—but it should and can be prepared to fight evil; a free people is only ready to resist aggression when the Christian virtues flourish, for a man of character in peace is a man of courage in war.

In a sense I have made two books: one, which was scribbled down in an army note book during the last war, is an epitaph of a battalion of the professional army of 1914, so that I have become jealous of its integrity. I have altered nothing in my diary even when it has not worn well with time. It is a record of changing moods; sometimes fresh from some more personal loss I have written as though I were a pacifist and war was sheer waste, sometimes it is plain that I held war to be the ultimate test of manhood. I wrote to fill the day and to save myself from the awful sameness of those years of trench warfare. As a doctor I have not been taught to share my feelings with others and now I am a little put out to find in print the intimate metabolism of my own mind.

The other I have written when I could; the last chapter was finished in a flying boat above the Atlantic ocean, and I am writing now in a bomber by a port-hole through which if I stand I can see far below me the Libyan desert. It was written for the soldier and the sailor so that I have shunned the language of the professional psychologist, but I cannot escape from the discipline of a life spent mostly in the isolation of facts, and if I have been at pains to erase from these pages the marks of my calling, the book is documented. The casual reflections on mustard gas grew out of nearly a year's work at Boulogne, and the view that modern war has signally failed to make cowards out of sound stock was built up, step by step, during the years that I was on the staff of a hospital for nervous diseases and saw the remnants of that struggle.

The two books have become one—the first is only used to illustrate the second—yet there still hangs around the whole a kind of dual nature. When my feelings as a man were at white heat they were always coming under the cold scrutiny of an eye trained in measurement, behind which the scientific way of life, with its passion for exactitude, pruned and purged.

The reader may sometimes wonder why, at a time when all his thoughts and hopes and fears are fixed on this war, I so often break the narrative while I ask him to live again through the experiences of the last war. But I have kept only those parts of my diary which throw light on the life of a soldier on active service in any war. Besides in war there is nothing which is new. The soldier at Waterloo saw a cannon ball coming straight for him; he could have avoided death by taking a step to one side but he did not move. If we knew why he stood fast and what he felt, it might help to anchor to his post the soldier whose ears are filled with the rising screech of the dive bomber.

If courage were common there would be no purpose in this book. But is courage common? That question haunts the pages of my diary: as time passes it changes in character. At first the question is clothed in something of the romance of those early days. Are there many adventurers left in England? And then at Ypres before the second winter doubt began to creep in until one day I had asked "Is this our modern equipment for meeting great adventures?" The war dragged on; the regular soldier began to disappear— after the Somme we belonged in everything but name to Kitchener's Army; the old confidence was replaced by a new concern for the battalion. I no longer had the heart for general speculations, but only for what might help to hold men to the task in hand, until in the third winter I wrote "There is a limit to the number of good men any race can furnish." And then with an air of finality "The morale of all armies broke sooner or later." I can find little in my diary to support the comfortable creed that all men in France were heroes. A few men had the stuff of leadership in them, they were like rafts to which all the rest of humanity clung for support and for hope.

After a quarter of a century I am driven to ask again "Is courage common?" I find it difficult now, living in soft security, to speak from the bench. Twice in my lifetime I have seen boys grow to men, only to be consumed by war, and I have come to think of this almost every day. War is only tolerable when one can take part in it, when one is a bit of the target and not a pensioned spectator. Yet when the death of husband or son or brother has grown distant, and the world is free to think again without impiety that courage is not common, men will remember that all the fine things in war as in peace are the work of a few men; that the honour of our race is in the keeping of but a fraction of her people.

We came to exalt courage. Was this man staunch in battle? That was the acid test to which every soldier in France was put. And now because courage is rare, because it alone stands between us and the ruin of our cause, we must once more acknowledge and confess the primacy of courage. This book is an attempt to unravel the behaviour of men in war, to explain how it comes that young men are ready to die that "there may be song for the men of after time".

12 May, 1943.

Chapter One

Of how imagination helps some men and destroys others

At Armentières, one day in 1914, when the First Battalion of the Royal Fusiliers was in billets, Wickham who commanded "D" Company told me that one of his sergeants was out of sorts. I found him sitting staring into the fire. He had not shaved and his trousers were half open. He seemed a morose fellow; I could get nothing out of him. Wickham did not want to send him sick, away from the battalion, besides he did not appear to be ill. We agreed to give him a rest, to let him stay in his billet till the battalion came out of the trenches. But next day when everyone had gone up the line he blew his head off. I thought little of this at the time; it seemed a silly thing to do. I knew nothing then of the tricks war can play with men's minds. In those early days of the first German War we—the Company officers and I—did not bother about men's minds; we did what we could for their bodies. We did not ask whether a man was wearing well or if he would last. Of course he would last, why shouldn't he?

Months later after the corrosion of nearly a year in the Ypres salient I was less certain. The heavy shelling at Ypres had helped to sort men, some who had been aggressive

1

enough at first with their blood up were wearing badly under stress. Early in 1916 I wrote:

> During operations in the South, the battalion was ordered to do a holding attack. The day before, Jimmy Grey came to me with some aches and pains, a little fever.
>
> "You know, Doc., I feel pretty rotten."
>
> "I'm sure you do but can't you see this business through?"
>
> He kept pacing up and down. He was full of his woes.
>
> "It will be all over in a few hours and then you can go down to the transport for a rest and stay there till you are fit."
>
> I grew more and more uncomfortable. That an officer should go sick like this was disquieting. I did not like it. It had never happened before. I wondered what the men would think. Jimmy had been well liked; he had a good eye and could play any ball game, besides he was the soul of good nature, but this business of war will have nothing to do with our old standards and values. There is one test, and by that he has been found wanting. In their hearts they know he has not made good and gradually as things have come to a head the subject has been dropped. Now the game was up; we should see no more of him.

: My job as a medical officer was to value the assets of the battalion—to take stock—to guard against depreciation. It was not much to ask of any man, but was I doing it? The sergeant at Armentières came into my mind; I began to wonder if I had been responsible for this fellow's end, if he should have been sent down the line sick. It was plain that he had found he could not face war and was not certain what he might do and had taken the matter into his own hands before he did something dreadful that might bring disgrace on himself and on the regiment. There was no selfishness in this. He was ready to go out of this world, but it must be in his own time and in his own way. I realised that I must live with the men, watch them, listen to them, get to know them, be their friend. I began to divide them into types.

There seemed to be four degrees of courage and four orders of men measured by that standard. Men who did not feel fear; men who felt fear but did not show it; men who felt fear and showed it but did their job; men who felt fear, showed it and shirked. At Ypres I was beginning to understand that few men spent their trench lives with their feet firmly planted on one rung of this ladder. They might have days without showing fear followed by days when their plight was plain to all the company. At other times they were possessed by the fear that they would be found wanting and branded as cowards, when in the toil and bloody sweat of trying to conquer themselves they would end by doing their job without a sign of fear. The story of modern war is concerned with the striving of men, eroded by fear, to maintain a precarious footing on the upper rungs of this ladder.

I have kept this crude division of the soldiers in the battalion into those four types because it helps me to answer two questions: Is the mind of the English soldier of 1914 and 1940, as far as his response to war is concerned, more sensitive, more alert than was the mind of his forebear in arms in the long chronicle of our wars? And, if so, have his leaders, assuming that they are aware of this change and its far-spreading implications, made full use of that knowledge in reviewing the rather stereotyped systems of discipline and training still in force?

I have to admit at the outset my very types are suspect, that the existence of natural courage (fearlessness as opposed to the courage of control) in any age may be challenged; that it is open to argument whether there is or ever has been anyone who does not feel fear. My own judgments of men in this respect even in the battalion with which I served for some years remained provisional. How liable to error then must be any scrutiny of the thoughts or want of thought of the soldiers who fought those far-off battles that are now hardly a legend! Yet if we have in our minds a clear image of what we mean by the yokel soldier and some knowledge of the times in which he fought, we may find in history grounds for deciding whether he was or was not the stuff out of which military reputations have been made. We shall find there evidence—as far as it is possible to identify in their ancient setting soldiers blessed by natural courage —that the armies of long ago were recruited, broadly speaking, from men who did not feel fear. Their courage seems to have had its roots in a vacant mind. Their imagination played no tricks. They drew no picture of danger for their own undoing. "If these English had any apprehension they would run away." Phlegm, that was the yokel's virtue as a soldier, it was the distinctive quality of his race.

Were the descendants of these yokel soldiers also the backbone of our army in France during the War which ended in 1918? I shall answer that this man who felt no fear, who was the substance of the armies of other days, was hardly to be found in that war, at any rate among officers. Where he survived he was an object of curiosity; men spoke of him with amusement and affection. My first Colonel, the pattern of the man who does not feel fear, was a being so singular in the 6th Division that he became a legend, as if men could scarcely believe what they had seen with their own eyes.

There are houses dominated by one personality, houses where no one else really matters. That role at battalion headquarters was filled by the Colonel. If he was in the room, everyone was kept on tenterhooks, wondering what he might say or do next. And if he happened to be out, all the time we were expecting his return. He was a soldier of the old style, if the phrase has any meaning nowadays when officers in mufti might pass for doctors, lawyers, or other folk who live by the public favour. He was a soldier because his father had been in the Service, and his grandfather and all his line. This grandfather had fought in Spain; it was not difficult to get into the way of thinking that the Colonel had been there too. His mental processes were not easily followed. When a man came before him on a charge he was convicted "pour encourager les autres". A trench to him was but another billet to be inspected for empty tins and stray equipment, in his mind it stirred up no tactical problems. For him the people who emptied tea leaves in odd corners were the real enemy. That was a problem he could deal with.

Maps were his pet aversion, especially trench maps. They were, he believed, the invention of the people behind who had nothing better to do. They conveyed very little to him; they did not help him to picture anything. He loathed all paper. One morning a gunner came into the mess and pulling out a map, asked the Colonel if he would mind marking the line which the battalion held. He stood gazing at the map, his broad flat face a little sulky and quite without intelligence, and presently placed his paw, fat, hairy and with mere stumps for fingers, where it covered the greater part of Northern France, then with a rude and impatient gesture he moved away and began rapidly to describe the ground as he must often have seen it in his travels overland, for he had the horseman's eye for country and was not one to wait for darkness to cover his wanderings. Yet this man who was a byword among the men for the risks he took, when he sighted a brigade orderly coming up the road on his push-bicycle, began to fume and fret. "Damn him," he growled, "what's wrong now?" And before the adjutant had time to read the message, he had snatched it from him. He was not sure of his job, so he was uncertain of his temper.

No one could remember that he was ever sick or

sorry; when anyone fell ill the Colonel plainly could not understand it though he was at bottom good natured. He made of each day a physical achievement, getting up before anyone else to turn out the servants. Immediately he had breakfasted he shouted to his man to remove the things, and when we came in like guilty children, the old fellow gave the impression that he was out for trouble, with his sturdy legs planted wide apart and his fat fists buried in the deep pockets of his riding breeches. But generally he turned his back on us, holding an old and coloured handkerchief with both hands where it might dry above the fire. Then he got into his trench kit and set off alone by some overland track that he had discovered was mostly dead ground. He wore an old brown balaclava drawn down on his head, that gave his broad flat features a look of some Lapland hunter. Across his shoulders he threw a waterproof sheet which he secured below his chin with a bit of string, and carried in his hand a long pole. He hurried over the sodden fields, but when he came to a particularly exposed place he stopped, and pulling out his knife began to remove great lumps of mud from his shoes, which he wore with stockings in all weathers, holding that gum-boots made him slow. If the Boche reminded him of his existence by a little sniping, he went on scraping. He is sure to be hit one day, people said, playing the fool like this, but nothing happened. The men grinned as he jumped into the trench, though he had never been known to praise anyone and mostly went about finding fault.

His groom and his batman passed most of the day in sleep, but still he kept them in his service whatever they did or did not do, more from the natural conservatism of his mind than from any sentiment or mutual attraction. One night, so the tale goes, on the march up from the Aisne, the Colonel was walking at the head of the battalion followed by his groom, along a road that ran between high hedges, when without warning the Germans opened fire apparently from the next field. The battalion subsided into the ditch almost without orders, leaving this groom sitting on his black pony in the bright moonlight, quite motionless and unmoved, being like his master without imagination. On these occasions the Colonel would mount a great horse and then he appeared almost attractive, so becoming are men's actions when they are second nature.

When darkness had fallen on the town he was sure to burst in again, and begin immediately to fuss about the mail. When it was sorted he stood by the fire, which now and then he kicked into life, and read his letters by the light of a candle that he held in his other hand. After dinner he spread out the *Morning Post* which made up his literature. Presently sleep overcame him; his face flattened out like a boxer's a little redder now with the wind and rain. Gradually his head fell forward till it rested on his hands, and nothing was visible but the top of his head, bald and polished like a bladder. From time to time he woke himself with a snort and looked up, blinking, in a stupid and dazed way. When he had done this many times he got up quickly and pouring out some brandy, drank it neat. Jerking out good-night, he shut the door, just as an awkward boy leaves the room.

I have rescued from my diary this sketch of a type that is vanishing to give reality to the man who does not feel fear. Yet one day the Colonel said to me that communication trenches were bad for morale. Did he find that out for himself? Was that grim old man in his wanderings overland in broad daylight and in full view of the Boche playing a part like the rest of us? Was the distinction between the Colonel and the man who while admitting that he felt fear, did not show it, a mere matter of candour?

I cannot answer. That he was less sensitive to danger than most men must have been plain to all who knew him. This freedom from fear—absolute or relative as you will—was in him the outcome of the slow working of his mind, the torpor of his imagination. But there are men who are apparently fearless though their minds are active; these men—I can count on one hand those I have known—have in the jargon of my calling a higher threshold to fear as others have a higher threshold or are less sensitive to pain. But do they really feel less than we do or have they attained a peak of control which is beyond our reach? In Cairo recently I asked Lord Gort, a V.C. and one of the five I had placed apart in this lonely breed of men, whether he ever felt fear. "Of course," he answered at once, "all animals feel fear. When I used to go back to the trenches after some time out of the line I had to adjust myself, and even now when I return to Malta after a few days here without any bombing it will be different for a little."

Is there then anyone who does not feel fear? Those who lived in the trenches for a long time may answer by recalling some happy soul who did not appear to be conscious of danger, and had never had to make an effort to carry on. For months, perhaps, he ballooned about envied by all, happy and unconcerned. Perhaps he was killed or wounded and was remembered as a man without fear. But if the enemy was less merciful and he was left on his feet, the frailty of the rest of men overtook him; time had stolen away from him his peace of mind that came from a certain vacancy which had always passed for courage. Recklessness may have been the first sign of trouble brewing, the rest quickly followed. When his friends were gone his mind began slowly working, for the first time he saw danger and then he broke. This fellow and the Colonel were not after all exceptions to the rule: no man can go on for ever, sooner or later all men feel fear.

In support of that verdict I shall call in evidence Sir John Fortescue, the historian of the British Army. He writes

It is, I believe, a fact that even the bravest man

cannot endure to be under fire for more than a certain number of consecutive days, even if the fire be not very heavy.

Commander Holbrook, a sailor who won the V.C. in the last war by an act of extreme bravery, has also told us

If you are a captain of a submarine and you have nerves, you have no right to be a captain. All the men's lives depend on you. . . . I used to feel in an awful funk at times. It is absurd to say you do not. I have yet to meet the fellow who will lie in his ship at the bottom of the sea and be depth-charged and not suffer from cold feet. I felt this strain, but did not realise it at the time; but when you go back to harbour you must have rest. You feel like a washed out rag. With all those mines around you do not want a depth charge too close to send you to glory.

If natural courage—the courage of insensibility—is almost extinct among officers, was that apathy as rare among the men? Were their hides no thicker? It was at least true that the change in them was less complete. There were whole battalions recruited among yokels such as the 9th Sussex, where the men did not seem to think at all. They came from a part of England that had not been touched, or at any rate had been but slightly affected by the industrial age, which elsewhere was slowly eating away at this happy remnant of another and a simpler time. The strength of the yokel soldier lay in his obstinate refusal to recognise danger when it was all around him.

I do not doubt there were scattered through the armies in France during the Great War many descendants of the insensitive heroes of other days. But they were relics of a ruder time. The conditions of to-day were altogether unfriendly to the apathetic straw-chewing fellow who was so staunch in battle because he never stopped to reason, to measure the odds, or to reflect on his own chances of survival. The day was gone when a lot of healthy animals could be thrown at some strong place for any vague reason or want of reason. We were moving away from that primitive valour, fumbling for a type of soldier whose courage was a thought-out thing.

I do not suppose that change will be questioned, but it is just possible that there are some who may claim that this change in the type of soldier came about less abruptly than I suggest and that it was forced on our attention by conscription. If I could say when this change occurred it would help me to say why it occurred, and what social conditions in the life of the people brought it about. It does not help in dating the disappearance of the man with natural courage that his descendant, the common soldier, who did his job in spite of feeling fear, has most consistently failed to catch the historian's eye. Sir Philip Sidney, Sir John Moore and their kind certainly bear witness that a crude want of feeling has not been our only equipment for meeting great adventures. But were they only sports deposited by fate in the midst of a host of gaping yokels? At any rate the feeling man, the man who felt fear but did not show it; the man who felt fear and showed it, and yet did his job, are most difficult to trace in our military annals. If I had to hazard an explanation why it is so difficult to find their tracks on those old battlefields it would be that such men stayed at home. Until the Great War, which became the business of millions, willing and unwilling, our battles were fought by picked men, soldiers of fortune. Conscription when it came hustled to arms a lot of quivering creatures who would never have gone to war of their own free will. If I am wrong, if feeling men went to the wars the motive that made them fight—often the driving force of religion— dulled their fear. They no more dreaded death. A simple faith fortified or hid their frailty. If this be the explanation, that faith has gone, without it we can no longer masquerade as men without fear. We are stripped and known for what we are.

At any rate few will question the change. Men suffered more in the last war, as it seems to me, not because it was more terrible but because they were more sensitive. It was not that the horror of battle had been raised to a pitch no longer tolerable, but that their resistance to fear had been lowered. Some subtle change in men's nature which was not the effect of the war, but of the conditions of life before the war, had taken place, that left them unprotected, the sport of battles.

But is this change in the texture of our minds necessarily a handicap in war? To such a question there is, I think, no very satisfactory answer. I wish I could believe that in reading the soldier's mind and its response to war I had been free from error. Unfortunately my diary permits no such complacency. This page taken from it was written at a time when I was disturbed lest the softness that had crept into man might impair his efficiency as a soldier and I was still uncertain whether imagination was a help or a hindrance in war. Late in 1915 I wrote:

Is it a secret purpose that steels men's hearts in France, or is it only apathy that takes away their sense of reckoning?

Captain Bairnsfather's drawings are a successful attempt to fix the atmosphere of the trenches. What they depict is unconscious and protective, a way of looking at things which alone makes it possible to carry on. The 'sticker' is just one who has contrived to cut off those messages from the outer world that reach the brain at times like these and threaten its balance. His business is to become insensitive, to give up thinking. The wise man lives only for the hour.

I used to think that only primitive men were adapted for this final test, that imagination which is the secret of supremacy in peace was merely a handicap in war. It did not help a man in the trenches; to picture what might happen to himself and others was the most perilous thing he could do.

And then this note, written a year later.

The outstanding personal successes in this battalion at any rate have been among imaginative men. They were able to see more fully than others could that there was no decent alternative to sticking it and to see this not in a hot moment of impulse but steadily through many months of monotony and trial. They understood on what terms life was worth while.

Barty Tower who left us at Ypres nearly two years since to take over a Kitchener battalion has been killed in front of the Boche wire in some divisional show. It is not what happens out here but what men think may happen that finds the flaw in them, yet it is the thinking soldier who lasts in modern war. Barty had no flaw, he had the finish and polish of all old things. The history of his family was written over his mind like a crossed letter and all his thoughts had been inherited with his small round head, his thin delicate features, his long nervous hands. He believed everything worth doing had been done by a small sect, a privileged caste, where the only people who really mattered lived shut off from the world. He believed too that war was a special occasion in which certain calls were made on that sect. He had always felt that, but these calls had not proved to be the things he had expected. War had not meant going out in front of his men in the face of the enemy. It had meant waiting, one long nightmare of suspense, it had meant living in a ditch, the foreman of a gang of diggers and carriers, it had meant noise and stench and vermin and dirt. In the retreat from Mons and in the first battle of Ypres the people he knew had fought in their own way, their training told. It was just what he had expected. But a new time had come of machines, of miscalculation, of doubt, and among the survivors the defects that were the fruit of that training became clear to himself and to others. There were people who were not real soldiers at all, who ventured to criticise the old army, and some of these people seemed quite useful at this game.

Before the war we must have had little in common; doctors to him were people who did things for one like chemists and other tradesmen, things for which one paid. Yet one day he told me laughing that whenever he heard a shell coming he saw himself blown to bits, an arm here, a leg there. I often wondered how many could have paid that price, and said he must be living on his capital and that this does not go on for ever. But in the end he went out undefeated, in my heart I believe he was invincible.

In the unending struggle between fear and the idea greater than fear he could find no rest, no moment's peace. He saw danger multiplied as a child sees its face magnified in some distorting mirror, but he saw too through this same mirror the idea greater than fear till it came to be his religion.

Men like Barty who drew a picture of danger the moment they met it so complete, so terrific that it seemed no mortal man could stay to face it, have outlasted everyone. In their lonely struggle, hidden away from the sight of others, they drew on the past; it was as if the dead of their race had spoken to them and awaited them.

If imagination helps some men it destroys others; when allowed to run riot it becomes a menace to the soldier but when controlled by character it blossoms in a Barty Tower.

It is tempting to enquire whether our Generals in the last war were aware of this change in the soldier's mind? Their attitude to his psychology was like the lip service which some pay to a religion that is no longer part of their lives and has ceased to affect their conduct. They knew, it has always been a military axiom, that a man's will to

B

fight is the ultimate arbiter of battles and that this is governed by the thoughts however elementary which pass through his head. But when they tried to follow and influence those thoughts their notions of how to do it were so simple as to be almost disarming. To cultivate the aggressive spirit—they attached much importance to this—they believed that men must be made to see red, and the only way they could think of goading them to the required pitch of ferocity was to picture the enemy as infamous. It did not occur to them that there is a vein of magnanimity in the average Englishman which gives him a second wind in war, inoculating him against selfishness, the ultimate foe. He finds no help at all in blackening the enemy. They forgot, too, that men of our race grow in adversity; that grave news binds them into one happy company. The staff thought any yarn, any bit of optimism, good enough for the consumption of the troops; the contempt became mutual.

Our Generals might, of course, argue that Napoleon's recipe for moulding the thoughts of his soldiers, if we may judge from his bulletins, was as simple as their own; he believed his armies were only capable of a few primitive emotions which he could manipulate in his sleep. It was astonishing, he remarked, "what men would do for a bit of ribbon". This was sufficient for his time. It is hardly adequate for a democracy which has been taught for twenty years that war is a criminal folly which solves nothing, for men who will only fight as a painful duty. The cynicism of the past, the manipulation of the facts and minds of men by those who believe in nothing must be replaced by a fixed faith in the ultimate betterment of man. Only a leader with a vein of nobility in his character can understand what is passing through the mind of the citizen soldier of this war.

To that soldier I have to say something which is not easy to say from the touch line. In the armies of the democracies where duress is used with forbearance there are sometimes soft spots and we have been told there is evidence that in the case of some of the troops at Singapore and Tobruk the enemy found some of these spots. I should not myself be disposed to place on such facts as have been established too heavy a weight of inference. It would be tempting to enquire how far the scepticism of the age and the decay of principle have contributed to any change that may have taken place. But what evidence of change do we possess which would bear even a casual scrutiny? The spectacle of crabbed age bemoaning the deficiencies of youth is not new. "I do not myself believe that this age is either less spiritual or more sordid than its predecessors." That was said by Mr. Arthur Balfour in the year I became a doctor. To that faith I still subscribe.

Nevertheless there are circumstances mostly arising out of the last war which have confused and perplexed the fluid mind of youth. This generation was brought up at the feet of their fathers who served in the citizen army of the last war. They were nurtured on tales of Passchendaele and of the Somme; they were prepared for any story of ineptitude. Is it so strange that it should stand aghast at the folly and waste of a war which had solved nothing and was only the prelude to another and vaster conflict in which they themselves were asked to play their part? It does not seem to me that we seniors are in a position to criticise our juniors.

A short time ago the Allies had taken only fourteen Japanese prisoners; they asked to be shot or to be allowed to shoot themselves. They could never return to Japan. When they were posted as missing they were in the eyes of their countrymen dead. If this generation is to die as stalwartly as any Japanese or German thug it is in need of a certain way of thinking. "Nature", Emerson warned us, "has made up her mind that what cannot defend itself shall not be defended." This book is concerned how that way of thinking is set up and thereafter kept inviolate.

Chapter Two

Cowardice

By cowardice I do not mean fear. Fear is the response of the instinct of self-preservation to danger. It is only morbid, as Aristotle taught, when it is out of proportion to the degree of the danger. In invincible fear—"fear stronger than I am"—the soldier has to struggle with a flood of emotion; he is made that way. But fear even when morbid is not cowardice. That is a label we reserve for something that a man does. What passes through his mind is his own affair.

There are acts which are by no means easy to excuse that nevertheless do not offend against military law. A man might have fallen short of the standards he had set himself, he often fell far short, but he was spared that final catastrophe. He had seen men go till none were left of those who had fought with him. He had gazed upon the face of death too long until exhaustion had dried him up making him so much tinder, which a chance spark of fear might set alight. He was forced at last to see the odds, by a wound perhaps, by a bad part of the line, by gas, by an unhealthy atmosphere in the mess, by some narrow escape that led him to ask can such luck last, by a hundred little things each in itself of small account. Yet he was not broken. There was no dramatic failure in the line, no act of cowardice in the face of the enemy; only a subtle undermining of his will which led him to stay in England where illness or a wound had honourably taken him, to seek out jobs where he might exist in safety, or to do something which would not excite the open disapproval of his fellows, though his own conscience was for ever calling him back to the line. All this may be indefensible but it is not cowardice.

What then is this sickness of the mind which leads up to complete and final failure to play the part of a man? When we say that a soldier has been guilty of cowardice we are making use of a term to which the dread penalty that awaits a man convicted of that crime has lent precise and limited meaning.

The Army Act lays down that a man is guilty of cowardice when he displays "an unsoldierlike regard for his personal safety in the presence of the enemy" by shamefully deserting his post or laying down his arms.

Can war in time make any man a coward? Is it a calamity due to some horrible experience and therefore something which might happen to anybody who was in that place at that time? Is it pure chance that some are branded as cowards while others win fame as heroes? These are questions that may well stop the youth of England at their tasks, and make them think. For what peace of mind can any man have if his honour is no longer in his own keeping? The hour cries for an answer.

When I ask can war make any man a coward it is no answer to point to men who were cowards before they were soldiers. Such men went about wearing labels for all to read. From the first they were plainly unable to stand this test of men. They had about them the marks known to our calling of the incomplete man, the stamp of degeneracy. The whole miserable issue could have been foretold, the man was certain to crack when the strain came.

In the spring of 1917 an officer with large irregular

features came to the battalion. We were in a quiet part of the line, but he began to crack at once. Soon he kept to his dug-out like an animal, he could not be lured into the trench. A few nights later I found him in my dressing station, huddled up on a chair oblivious of the presence of men of his own company; his face was working and there was a wild look in his staring eyes. Here drink at work for many years had destroyed the man. Fear flourished in that sodden soil like a fungus, and all that we mean by a man was dead.

There were others who were as plainly worthless fellows. One without moral sense had taken a commission under the shadow of compulsion. His second day in the trenches he came to me with a note from his Company Commander asking me to remove him. That fellow sitting there with his head in his hands at the bottom of the trench could do no good to the men of 1916. He showed none of the extreme signs of fear, he was just a worthless chap, without shame, the worst product of the towns. There was a rush on at the time and he got away. Later I heard that on the boat he was full of his doings with the battalion; England would give him a better hearing.

Still less is it an answer to my question to instance men who were reduced to cowardice by physical hurt. There were men of stout heart who were brought to that plight by the blast of a shell which damaged their brains. These men had come out of some rending explosion with their skins intact but with dishevelled minds. The story was always the same. A shell had burst close by. Moreover up to that moment their record was free from blemish. When a soldier was frightened out of the trenches by his thoughts the rest of the company had been prepared for his disintegration by the signs of "wind" known to the observant. But in this man there had been no warning of coming trouble, the break up was sudden and complete. Without a careful record of the man's carriage before he was shelled it is often difficult to recognise commotional shock—the name given by my calling to this condition to distinguish it from emotional shock in which a man is frightened by his thoughts. It was a long time before we doctors understood what had happened. But from the first the men made up their minds that their mate was not frightened, he was hurt. They could not bear to think that he might be bundled back to the base with men who were afraid of their own shadow, when a few minutes back he had been one of themselves.

Yesterday in the grey light of a winter morning a stretcher bearer came to my dug-out.

"It's Sergeant Turner, sir," he said this as if we had already lost the war.

"Is he hit?" I asked.

The man hesitated. "No," he answered. "You see, sir, it burst almost on the top of him, a Jack Johnson. It's a miracle, I says, as he's here at all."

I found the Sergeant standing in the trench. He looked at me as if he had something to say but he said nothing. His lip trembled and he was trying to keep his limbs still. He appeared dazed by what he had been through and by this end to everything. He asked me to send him to transport for a day or two, he thought he would be all right soon. But it was plain to me the game was up and he was done. When this sort of thing happens to a good fellow it is final. One of my people brought him a tin of tea. They seemed to feel his position as if it had happened to themselves. This man came out with the battalion, was wounded and came back to us unchanged; he seemed proof against all the accidents of this life, he stood in the Company like a rock; men were swept up to him and eddied around him for a little time and ebbed away again, but he remained. And now he must be hurried away to the base to a shell-shock hospital with a rabble of misshapen creatures from the towns.

Where pluck was concerned the men made no mistake,

and so as time passed, an officer who knew his men, when he heard a good fellow had gone in this way would ask how far away the shell had burst. He did not believe in shell shock but this was different: the men were right. Further back where doctors could do their tests, it would be found perhaps that an ear drum had been broken by the blast of a shell or that there was blood in the fluid removed from the spinal canal, which were tokens of the damage done to their poor brains. Such a man had not been defeated by his thoughts; he was hurt as men with broken limbs are hurt, though there was no scratch upon him.

Sometimes I heard of stout fellows in other units who had cracked; and when I asked how it came about they could tell me nothing; they assumed it was the work of time. I remember one good soul, the last of five brothers, whom I found at a base hospital, a shaking remnant of a man, with the D.C.M. to puzzle the curious. "I think, sir," he said, "when Tom went it did it." The death of his last brother had seemed to him a final warning that fate had fixed upon his family and meant to destroy it. The end however had come when a big shell had burst near him, and I found myself wondering if it was a train of thought or physical hurt that brought him there.

It cannot be denied that any man may be brought down to the coward's level by physical hurt, but it is safe to affirm that "commotional shock" leading to cowardice was not common in the last war. If it had been, and we had often been left in doubt whether men's actions were involuntary or not, then the social meaning of courage as set forth in this book would have to be jettisoned. It is however possible that the blast of the modern bomb may lend an importance to commotional shock in this war which it did not possess in the last. But the two conditions—emotional shock and commotional shock—can be kept apart and it is vital to keep them so, for when a man is hit he deserves more consideration than when he is frightened. If this is forgotten, the men's sense of what is right and just is offended.

I am even now not at the end of my exceptions. When a soldier's resistance to fear has been lowered by sickness or by a wound the balance has been tilted against him and his control is in jeopardy at any rate for a time. The wounded soldier has just visualised danger in a new and very personal way. It has been brought home to him as never before that he is not a spectator but a bit of the target, just as a doctor after attending head wounds may come to dislike bullets pinging past his ear more than any shells. His discovery of danger comes at the moment when an honourable alternative to death is held out. There is a welling up of the instinct of self-preservation which is now unopposed. He is no longer interested in his unit or in the battle. If his wound is not serious he may be in such a hurry to get out of range that he does not go to the regimental aid post but hastens to the field ambulance, a long way back.

Even illness may bring a man to the verge of defeat. I can recall a personal and disconcerting example of the stealthy attack of physical unfitness so that all at once it became more difficult to do one's job. In the summer of 1915, when we were waiting in Sanctuary Wood to go into action at Hooge, I had a passing fever; when night came and spare bullets hit the trees with a dull thud I had to take hold of myself that I might walk a hundred yards through the wood. Sir Arthur Hurst has told us that the majority of the soldiers evacuated from Gallipoli in November and December, 1915, were suffering from dysentery; many were also jaundiced. Their exhaustion was profound. When they arrived at Lemnos few of them could carry their packs on the march, they had to stop and rest every hundred yards. Almost to a man, he affirms, their nerves were ajar.

I have still to admit that there are tempered soldiers proved in battle who have been stripped of their self control by some intense emotional shock. Their will power has been used up, they are spent for the moment. But such men if happily they are not put to the test while their guard is down rapidly recover. Their will is once more equal to its task.

In the early spring of 1915 I chanced to be alone in my dug-out towards evening during heavy shelling when one of my stretcher bearers came in, his face working; the man was drivelling. A corporal with him explained that this bearer and three others had been carrying a man on a stretcher when a shell caught them and literally splashed him with bits of the other three bearers. He himself escaped without hurt. Now he seemed done. I sent the corporal away and resolved to keep the bearer until things were quieter. I got him to lie down on the stretcher on which I slept. Almost at once to my great wonder he fell asleep. It occurred to me that there might be an outside chance of saving this fellow the mishap of going to the base with shell-shock. I dropped a blanket down so that he was hidden and made him some hot stuff to drink. He slept for nearly twenty-four hours. When he awoke he seemed all right. He went out with me next day and never looked back again. Fatigue, loss of sleep and the shock of witnessing the death of the other bearers had for the moment used up his will power. I remember too that Brousseau, a doctor in the French Army, relates how many of his comrades were annihilated before his eyes. The survivors, veterans, found themselves absolutely incapable of making up their minds what to do. All danger was past but their will power was exhausted. This lasted half an hour, at length self-control came back.

Now that I have put aside those who were frightened before they heard a shot, who limped into war half-men, and those who were undone because they were hurt in mind or body, let me ask once more: can war in time make any man a coward? My answer is that these men apart, the last war most signally failed to turn men of sound stock into cowards. When men had been at the mercy of their instincts, when they had given up the effort to control fear and had abandoned themselves to their impulses, there was something in their make-up that made them less willing or less able to behave unselfishly. It was not fear, many who had been most miserably afraid had done splendid, memorable things. It was not the evil chance of time or place, the hellish bombardment, or war would be a lottery in which the unlucky drew the stamp of cowards. No: it was only bad stock that brought defeat.

A verdict of that kind, so reassuring to the young soldier —"the thing in the world I am most afraid of is fear"—does not clash with my other finding that no man has an unlimited stock of courage and that when this is done he is finished. The reserves of a man of character may be nearly spent, he may have fallen far short of the standards he had set himself, but he has always been able in my sight to stave off defeat, to stop short of cowardice in the precise and limited sense in which that word is used in this chapter.

Chapter Three

The birth of fear

The physician tries to put a name to mortal disease so early in its course that it can be extirpated. So must the soldier deal with the dread malady of fear. By fear I do not mean the state of apprehension that may take hold of any man when he meets danger first, which is no more than a natural concern how he may fare when put to the test of war. Fiction and the personal records of earlier wars have gathered a list of unpleasant sensations which we are led to believe attack a man when he comes under fire for the first time, and which he discards and leaves behind him as the conditions become more familiar. Of these physical signs of fear, the dry mouth and the rest, I know nothing.

Even when I have had to force myself to do things, they have been absent. The first time I was shelled I was not rattled. When I had got the wounded away I ate heartily, and I remember being filled with compunction that I could be so callous. Perhaps the wounded had given me something to do, something to think about. Yet I can recall every detail without opening my diary. For weeks after, while we were in those trenches, it was impossible to leave the farm that was battalion headquarters without passing three small wooden crosses planted at the back, in a spot where graves could be dug by day out of sight of the Boche; each cross bore the date 20th December, 1914, to jog the memory. Under that date I made this note on fear:

It is unusual to get shells on the back areas in these parts, and we have been living above ground in a farm perched on a little hill, where we can see the German trenches and be seen from them. This morning the Boche began shelling the farm. I put down my paper and went to look after the sick, mostly men with trench feet, so that it was a slow business getting them out of the barn. I shepherded them as quickly as I could into a sort of cellar, only three feet of which was underground. There we sat upon the straw, listening to the sound of falling bricks and slates when a shell happened to hit the buildings. The talking had ceased, and in the dim light it seemed as if those shadowy figures had been just roused from their sleep and were listening and waiting for something to happen. A shell seemed to burst in the passage, and another just outside the grating which let in what light there was in the cellar. And then there was a flash of light, a sudden terrific noise, a lot of fumes, then darkness again. There was some shuffling, a moment's silence and the sound of plaster falling from the ceiling. Perhaps we were going to be buried—and then another shuffle as several men jumped up and bolted for the stairs. The fumes cleared; most of the men were still squatting on the floor; they grinned at me in a friendly, paternal, and rather approving sort of fashion, but one poor specimen with a white face and a large Adam's apple sticking out of his scraggy neck stood irresolutely in the middle of the cellar, swallowing.

"Cheer up, sonny, you'll soon be dead," a big fellow said as he threw a fag to him. There was a hole in the wall of the cellar where the shell had come in, through which a patch of grey sky was visible. I foolishly expected another shell to come in at the same spot, and wanted to move out of the line of the hole, and had a feeling the Boche could see this hole and was watching it for any signs of life.

"If someone doesn't see to my leg I'll bleed to death, sir." The blood rushed to my face. I looked quickly round; Smith, the cook, and one of the signallers were kneeling as if in prayer, their heads in the straw, while the other signaller was curled up as if asleep. I thought they were rattled, but they were dead. By their side the orderly-room sergeant lay with his leg smashed, his great muscular thigh seemed as if it had been broken across one's knee. There were others wounded, and now that I had something to do, I forgot all about the shells and did not notice that the shelling had stopped.

The Adjutant called down from the open door: "All right, Doc?" and without waiting for an answer, said: "Is Smith there? Tell him we'll have lunch when it's ready. Get a move on," he said impatiently.

While we ate they talked about hunting; they did not once mention the shelling. But if I happened to say anything they listened with a friendly interest that I had not noticed before. And, in spite of the three dead men, I could not help feeling cheerful now that it was over. It was as if I had achieved something though I had done nothing.

When I write of the birth of fear I have in mind something more deeply rooted, that has nothing to do with the stage fright of the novice who does not know if he is going to act badly or well, something that is born of time and stress, which a man must watch lest it come to influence what he does. It appears only in men who have been scarred by months of war; unless the initial plunge is into a battle or intense shelling it may be months before the ordinary man has any trouble. His discovery of danger does not come at once; often it does not come for a long time. At first he has a strange feeling of invulnerability—a form of egotism

—then it is suddenly brought home to him that he is not a spectator but a bit of the target, that if there are casualties he may be one of them.

In this sense I find fear mentioned in my diary only once before the spring of 1915, and then only as we might describe a man seized with a fit in the street, something bizarre that was not part of our lives. But as the war dragged on, and fear was no longer an occasional and exotic visitor but a settler in our midst, I got into the habit of watching for signs of wear and tear, that a man might be rested before he was broken.

At Armentières there was a big curly-headed sergeant with a red face and an open smile who appeared quite indifferent to the war, if we can call that first winter in those parts war. He really commanded the company in those days. Later in the Ypres salient he handed to his officer every day a list of the wounded in his company. He must have known the odds, but he was never led to apply that knowledge to himself; it left him unmoved. He was so imperturbable on patrol that men liked going out with him. No harbingers of death and danger came to him on such ventures, for he was deaf, and could not hear bullets or any of those sounds which set men's brains working to their undoing.

Everyone spoke well of him and during the Somme he got the D.C.M. Then at Vimy all at once something happened. It was peaceful in those parts without much shelling, only "minnies" which made a big crater but did little harm. They were lobbed over from the German trench; you could see them coming; it was like waiting for a high catch in the long field. The men watched them and when they saw where they were going to fall they had time to dodge round the next traverse. This sergeant got into the way of watching them too; he seemed fascinated by them. Soon I discovered to my astonishment that they were doing him no good. As he stood with his eyes glued to the little dark object still high up in the air he began to think; it occurred to him that he had been a long time with the battalion. He began to go over in his mind what had happened to those who came out with him; he had been lucky, but could it last? A fortnight after we left Vimy he came to me sick. He got to England. It was as well; the war had been brought home to him at last: in my heart I marvelled that he had stayed so long. Those harmless "minnies" which were almost a joke had done what Ypres with its heavy shelling could not do. But happily he went in time and they who keep his memory know nothing of the last sickness of his mind.

Sometimes my task was not difficult. Early in the war a boy fresh from school joined the battalion; a nice-looking boy but with hardly any chin. His brother had been in the Regiment too, a good fellow they said, adding that if the lad was anything like him he would be an addition. But at Ypres I began to wonder if he would last. When something went wrong in the mess, or when Chang lost his temper, his eye blinked as if he had got dust in it, and the angle of his mouth twitched as if jerked by some invisible string. This boy would need watching. Yet he did his job, and as the months went by without anything happening my doubts were gradually lulled to rest. Then, after the Somme there seemed to be a change in him. Mike had gone now, and Jack; and Pat his closest friend, who always asked people where they hunted, had been sniped through the head. None were left but a few middle-aged rankers, men old enough to be his father. When he came to us he had been a shy reserved boy, who in the mess never expressed a view of his own. But now he began to get irritable at any little thing, sometimes even at nothing. One day he burst out "For God's sake, Johnson, can't you talk of something else than the bloody war," and without waiting for an answer rushed out of the mess. He was drinking more whisky, too, than was good for anyone. That twisting movement of the face, always the same movement, was never away for long now; there was trouble brewing. But when a staff job was mentioned he said the staff could go to hell; he would not listen when we spoke of sending him sick; he wanted to be transport officer, to have charge of the horse-lines, but there was no vacancy. I kept telling Hancock, who was commanding the battalion, that he must get him away to some job— any job; he said he would see about it, but time passed and nothing happened. Perhaps he liked having the boy about headquarters; he was the last of the old type. Perhaps he could not raise the energy to badger the people behind to find the lad a job. Then one day the boy was found in a fit. It was too late now, he was an epileptic.

At a time when all the people for whom I cared were being blotted out, one after another, it is strange how a little thing like that stuck. It was my job to get these fellows away in time, there was nothing else I could do. I wondered if I had become slack. I was always tired now. I resolved to watch more closely when times were bad; if I did, I felt something would surely tell me what was threatening.

Sometimes it was an accident that told me of a man's plight. There was a boy in the battalion who came to us from the flying people where he had been an observer for nearly a year. He was the gayest, most irresponsible creature who never seemed to take anything seriously. But one night I shared a dug-out with him and was roused from my sleep by his shouts and yells. I went to wake him from his dreams; then with my hand on his shoulder I stopped. He would not wish to share his secret with anyone. A week later while I still wondered what I might do, death came quietly to set him free. Sleep had let me into his secret, which he had kept hidden away through all those months at Ypres so that none knew of it. He knew fear, but he knew too it could never say to him do this and do that; the terror which dogs a man who has come to doubt his power to remain master of his ways was kept away from him by the pride and habit of his race.

Sometimes a company officer, more often a sergeant, was the first to see signals of distress. When the battalion was in trenches near Messines in the spring of 1916, Howard, who commanded one of the Companies, spoke to me about a subaltern who always seemed to be hanging round his headquarters. This boy had dark eyes under long lashes, a pink and white complexion, and a small fair moustache brushed away from his upper lip; when he laughed, which he did with little reason and in a nervous way, you could not help noticing his moist white teeth. The lad gave one the impression of unusual alertness. He looked consumptive, but I already suspected that his dry cough, which made people pause in their conversation until he had finished, and presently got a little on their nerves, was not unconnected with the war. One day coming round a traverse I met Howard. "The very man, Doc, I want you to vet this damned fellow." We found the boy in his dug-out. He made every possible excuse to put off my examination until we went out of the trenches, but Howard told him to get a move on. When the lad stripped we found he was wearing a coat of mail under his vest.

But even when I saw signs of fear it did not necessarily mean that a man should be scrapped forthwith. It might be no more than summer lightning, and the storm a long way off. One day, nearly a year after joining the battalion, while we were being shelled I found myself shivering. It did not immediately occur to me that it was connected with the shells, and as it was a cold day I put on my British warm. But the trembling did not cease. I grew perturbed and was relieved to discover that my plight had passed unnoticed. For days I went about with fear in my heart lest I should do something foolish when times were bad. Weeks passed and I think I had forgotten all about it, when one day during trench shelling I found the fire step shaking, and on looking up saw one of the sergeants standing a few yards away shivering like a reed in the wind. Yet we were agreed that we were not windy at the time. This ague may mean nothing.

I was for ever taking stock of character, but the task was beset with difficulty. I have seen this same sign allied with fear and yet it did not disturb me. Early in 1916 I wrote this note at Messines:

> During shelling he, Jack, looks just like a boy who is beginning an illness with shivering attacks, and in the frankest way he will tell you he is just petrified by the business. But I don't worry much about him, because in the intervals his mind is quite normal. He neither thinks too much of what is gone nor of what may come. He just gets as much out of life as he can. While this lasts he won't crack however much he is scared.

It is not everything to put a finger on the signs of fear; we have to weigh their inner meaning.

And yet there are signals of personal defeat which are like red lamps on broken roads, to these we must pay heed. I grew anxious when a man's speech began to betray him; when he was full of windy talk of what the Boche had done in the new sector the battalion was taking over, of some new gas. It was always about something which was going to happen; the wretched fellow must have known the mess would muzzle him if it could, but he seemed driven by some inner force to chatter incessantly of every calamity that could conceivably come to pass. It was as if he had come to terms with the devil himself, that if he could make others as windy, his life would be spared. How full of apprehension the fellow was; death came to him daily in a hundred shapes. This was fear in its infancy. It was a bad sign, for when a man talked like that, his self respect was going, and the battle was already half lost. It was just a matter of time. Such a man did the battalion no good for the disease was infectious; I was glad to get him away.

But sometimes the shadow of fear drove men in just the opposite direction, into sheer recklessness. And yet this recklessness meant different things in different men. Sometimes it was only an act of self-discipline whereby some too sensitive soul hoped to school himself or test his self-control. We had no need to bother about such a man; he would cast out the demon for himself before it devoured him; he would win through; his self-respect was intact.

At Armentières in the early part of 1915 the officers of "C" Company lived in the remains of a farm which had become part of the front line. When the Boche shelled the farm, which he did from time to time, Barty Price used to stand on the steps well above the level of the trench, while the bricks fell all around him. With his hands thrust into his coat pockets he looked just like a farmer who has come out at evening to question tomorrow's weather. This was the same man who had once confessed to me that he had taken a year to get over the South African War. It was his way of convincing himself that he would do his job. But recklessness in the insensitive man had another end; when he began to defy fate, when in the men's jargon "he was always asking for it", it was a sign he was in trouble. It was his own blunt way of telling us that he too was beginning to understand the meaning of war; that he too would soon be gone.

And there was the change in a man's manner. Hill, who commanded the battalion at the Somme, has lately told me that for days after we came out of the battle my irritability was a nuisance, though I remember nothing of it. But when I look back I see that something happened to me then and that I have never been quite the same since.

Then there is drink, a last crazy effort to get something out of life while it lasts. Was this fellow breaking because he was drinking or was he drinking because he was breaking? Was alcohol a cause or a symptom of defeat? Not that it mattered, for once that game began the man was done.

In the Navy, secretly exulting in the sagas of its own past, there are "happy ships" where the perfect harmony existing between the officers and their men seals their resolution. Likewise in the English professional army of 1914, which the Germans themselves called "a perfect thing apart", there were battalions which were more than usually resistant to the corroding effects of strain and battle. It is from such a battalion that I have taken my illustrations of the birth of fear. These men had resolved to do nothing to besmirch the name of the Regiment, however fearful they might be in their hearts. They would rather have gone out than own defeat. I do not doubt that in less seasoned troops, where the idea greater than fear had taken no very definite shape, and the preparation of the individual mind for sacrifice had in consequence hardly begun, the birth of fear may have taken on ruder shapes.

The first signs of strain are nowhere more faithfully observed than in the Royal Air Force to-day. I owe more than I can tell to the officers of that Force in command of the stations I have visited. These fellows are where they are because, in a ruthless service where seniority counts for little, they had proved capable in the air of quicker and tougher thinking than the rest. They see men at grips; they measure their purpose; while still in the twenties they are already old with experience. They know that the earlier a pilot's plight is detected the better the chance that he will eventually fly again as a fighting pilot. He should show no sign of fatigue when the time comes for him to be rested; he should grumble when he is not allowed to fly. They taught me that when a pilot's behaviour on the ground changes, when a lad who had been the life and soul of the mess becomes silent and morose, when he loses interest and zest, and becomes critical and bad-tempered, then it is too late to save him.

To this general statement I shall make one exception. In the half-hour immediately after landing, particularly after an eventful flight, we can learn much about a pilot's fibre from his manner and his way of telling his story; we may think that he is the worse for wear, but if he is rested he will come again. If a pilot is not wearing well he may show it physically; his eyes in particular often betray him, his ways, what he does with his hands. There may too be changes in his way of flying, which is as individual as his signature. The leader of a fighter squadron notices that a pilot flies higher, that he no longer possesses the offensive spirit. He has too much dash or too little. Without knowing it he is so concerned with his own safety that he has lost his concentration, and no longer keeps to his formation under fire or in bad weather, or he stays with the flight instead of finishing off his man. He no more wants to fly, though he will still go up.

It was when the battle of the Somme was smouldering out that James Birley came to the Flying Corps, then in its infancy. In this service at that time a doctor was the man who saw the sick, that was his function; he had no other. The experienced airman believed he knew "what his men could stand" as well as any doctor, and it was a tenet of his faith that a pilot, by the exercise of will-power, could and should endure the stress of flying indefinitely. Birley was aware that this faith outraged the facts, for the number of pilots who had broken down had begun to reach alarming proportions. He brought to this situation a mind mature and nurtured in science and a personality that opened all hearts. He taught young men of action to respect the scientific method, and the little he has left on record has never been better said. Especially in the search for fear he has told us what to look for and when to look for it.

Birley counted in seasons the months of a pilot's life—there are no years. In his spring he learns to fly and learns to fight. During the first two months of active service he is more likely to become a casualty than to inflict casualties on the enemy, he gains experience only too often at the cost of his life. This is the most critical stage of his career, for nearly three-quarters of the casualties sustained in battle and in accidents among flying officers during the years of 1917 and 1918 occurred among those with less than three months of active service. If he survives, the pilot enters upon the summer of his career, a period of confidence and self-assurance, of initiative and dash, of skill and wise discrimination, of success and achievement. His vulnerability is now comparatively slight and his military worth is at its zenith. The length of this phase depends on the stuff of which the individual pilot is made, on the character of his work, and on his success in carrying out that work. But these summer months must pass, and when autumn comes the picture of the pilot's distress is no different from that of a soldier or a sailor, only the colouring varies.

The tired pilot may under these circumstances complain of having lost some of his keenness; he has recently been dissatisfied with his work, and for the first time has begun to wonder when it will be his turn to go home; he has already been out over six months. He has not been quite sure of himself in the air lately, and, to make certain that his confidence for flying is unshaken, he has attempted to reassure himself by proving his ability to execute various manœuvres dangerously close to the ground; the result has not been a success. Perhaps it is all due to the mess having been unsatisfactory; he thinks the tone has gone down; anyhow, he has been off his food. He has only just recently recognised that he prefers to leave the mess after meals, and lie down and read a book in his own room. His sleep is less sound than it used to be; he takes a long time to get off, and has lately been dreaming. At first the dreams were not unpleasant, merely that he was making bad landings and getting laughed at. Then they began to worry him; he would dream of long-forgotten experiences in the trenches, or that he was "brought down" and taken prisoner; and, he hardly likes to mention it, but once he was "brought down" in flames, and woke up in terror shaking all over. His administrative work on the ground has been a labour instead of a pleasant duty; he has had a row with his sergeant, and he feels the "C.O." is losing faith in him. The new pilots from England are not altogether satisfactory; his responsibilities weigh heavily on him, and he thinks that the death of a member of his flight was avoidable, and perhaps it was his fault. He admits that he is conscious of having to force himself into the air, and is inclined when leading a patrol not to "go for" things which he would have done without hesitation a fortnight ago. Anyhow, the whole thing is a complete mystery to him, although he is sure it is only temporary and the doctor will give him something to put him right. And so, seeking for trivial causes in explanation of a fundamental change, reluctant to acknowledge what he dreads—what, moreover, he has publicly condemned in others—equivocating, pursuing false hopes, and evading the real issues, this eminently brave man will frequently conclude with the appeal, "Don't tell me it's 'wind up'."

Chapter Four

Moods

Moods expose the workings of the conscious mind, as dreams lay bare what has hitherto been hidden in the unconscious. Man passes through the whole gamut of emotions in war; I am content to call up a few moods, partly to find if they help to that understanding of human nature on which success in the conduct of war largely depends, and partly for the light they cast on our attitude to the enemy, to danger, and to human destruction.

We must practise a prudent economy in emotion in time of war if we are to remain sane. Where there is a lavish display of feeling the mind is not at peace; it is divided against itself. To give flesh and bone to this conflict I borrow a simple example from an army journal, the name of which I have forgotten—

A sentry is faced suddenly by a large body of the enemy, his lowest instinct of self-preservation acts, but before any movement of flight can take place the instinct for the preservation of the race has intervened and barred the way to self-indulgence. The voice of duty tells him that his own safety must be subordinated to that of the army of which he is a member. And this voice of the herd is backed by threats of physical and moral penalties.

This struggle in the mind of the sentry is everyman's war, and in that war he that findeth his life shall lose it. This clutching at safety gnaws at a man's heart and we can only help by strengthening the voice of duty which keeps him a man. It is necessary to fortify the mind so that it is reconciled to danger. And all that I have written of the care and management of fear is but an attempt to show how this can be done.

In the presence of danger man often finds salvation in action. To dull emotion he must do something; to remain immobile, to stagnate in mind or body, is to surrender without terms. Whereas movement, work of any kind, helps to deliver him from those feelings which are traitors to his better nature. In the last war, the man in the observation balloon, with little to do but sit in the middle of a target, was more liable to break down than the observer in an aeroplane, while the observer was more vulnerable than the pilot. To sit still under bombardment in the trench was more testing than to fight in the open.

It is not only the safety of our skins that upsets our peace of mind. From childhood we want to do things and are only restrained by the admonitions of our elders, and this conflict between the individual urge to sample life and the herd instinct divides men according to Trotter into two groups. The mentally stable skimming the surface of life deal with an uncomfortable piece of evidence by rejecting its significance. "These sensible, reliable men of middle age, with their definite views, their resiliency to the depressing influence of facts," still form the directing class in England. To their dominance are ascribed most of our troubles. However that may be in peace, it is plain that the emotional stolidity of the Englishman is a war-winning quality. When

I search my diary that I may measure the influence of leadership on events, I find only phlegm, a vast imperturbability in the face of death, which gave to a few sway over their fellows. They were not plagued with moods.

In certain minds, however, mental conflict leaves scars. These men are sensitive to experience. Their eyes have been opened to the vision of the cruelty which everywhere lies close below the surface of life. Yet deeply ingrained in them is the doctrine of the herd that things on the whole are fundamentally right. So there is a conflict in their mind which in peace time shows itself as outbursts of temper or as vagaries of disposition. We dismiss them as unstable, we label them degenerates. In war this overcharging with emotion may so handicap men that they may be branded as cowards.

This world that Trotter in *Instincts of the Herd in Peace and War* had created out of books and hard thought was not checked by the chill experience of war; a world cleft so sharply into the stable and the unstable is too tidy to fit the facts. I do not suggest that there is nothing in such a division of mankind, for I am not sure that it will not be invoked to explain the fall of France, when time lends perspective to the provisional judgments of to-day. But if it is true, it is not the whole truth. There were many feeling men who walked in purgatory in the last war, who yet contrived a mask so that they were accepted as imperturbable and were given the government of their kind. When their self-control wore thin they were prone to moods, which were the language in which they spoke to us of their distresses. Without a key to those moods the reader of war books stumbles on without a chart.

It is a platitude of war that the worth of no man, however able, is proven until it has been submitted to ordeal by battle; until his response to the havoc of war is known. The annihilation of thousands of his own people, the death of many of his friends may shake the foundations of all but the most stable. His faculties may be numbed, his wits frozen by the appalling carnage. A torpor affecting all his thoughts and actions may fall upon him, or his senses may be left raw by the horrid slaughter. During the battle of Passchendaele a very senior staff officer asked to be taken to the battlefield. His mind was saturated with all its details; his practised eye took in the scene. Suddenly he said to those with him "What is that stream there?" "That, sir," said an officer pointing to the map, "is this road." When the staff officer saw for the first time what he had asked his men to do, he broke down and wept bitterly.

Even those who appear to be untouched by the havoc of war may expose their inward scars to the observant. Haig, with the Somme and Passchendaele graven on his mind, found peace in a Scottish covenanter's idea of predestination. Like Cromwell, he believed he was a man of destiny sent by the Lord to carry out the appointed task, cost what it might.

If the medical officer with a battalion escapes the responsibility for military decisions which gamble in human life, nevertheless he too has his own distresses. It is not the wounds he binds which matter, it is when something has been destroyed in the make-up of a man that the bloody business of war comes home to him. With a background of casualties in his mind he is prone to think that the men are being treated as pawns in the game; he may question if all this loss of life is necessary. He begins to ask himself who is responsible.

The revolt in his soul is only a phase in the transition from the Julian Grenfell mood of eager enterprise (we went into the high adventure of 1914, our hearts singing) to a colder mood of stoical endurance for the sake of a purpose. After more than two years of this business no feeling man can escape a sense of pity, it has slowly replaced the chivalrous ardour which in 1914 took him into the Army. He sees, he must see, that war is a cruel and wasteful holocaust, though a necessary evil if men are to live in freedom. If it were otherwise, if the sensitive soldier who knows the horror and futility of war bottles it all up in his bosom, he will break the sooner.

So much is natural and inevitable. But when this revulsion against the cruelty of war takes the form of trying to fix the responsibility of this cruelty on generals it is quite another matter. That mood, so full of disappointment, weariness, and the surrender of illusions, has now become a search for scapegoats. There is a wavering in my purpose, the will to see this business through falters. I have printed this incident as it was written, in all its bitterness of spirit, as a warning. It was a lapse, perhaps a sign of wear and tear, and we must take heed of these signs, in whatever disguise they may appear.

Besides it is too late to draw up an indictment of war. It is not for a man with a battalion to sit in judgment on the folly of war in general or on the conduct of that campaign in particular; he may not be moved by pity nor cast down by the lot of a generation. He respects men whose principles prevent them taking up arms, but he himself has gone to war in the faith that there is no other way open to those to whom freedom of the mind is life itself. There he must remain. The rights of the individual have gone, he belongs to his men. He has accepted war, he must allow no mood, think nothing, do nothing, that may weaken his own purpose or the purpose of his fellows.

THE INSPECTION

The Division has been taken out of the line to rest—and the battalion is quartered at Fouquières near Bethune. Here the men sleep in barns or lofts where there is plenty of clean straw and roofs that leak less than usual; this they count luxury. It is not comfort we miss out here. It is easy after all to keep men physically fit, it is the mind that gets out of gear. I had hoped we should be billeted at Anezin, where the men would have been in cottages. They love mucking in with the inhabitants. Poor devils, they want occasionally to have a woman moving about the house, busy with cooking and with children while she answers their extraordinary lingo.

A few days ago, Hill, who is commanding the Ninth Sussex, sent me word that General Nivelle was coming to inspect the 73rd Infantry Brigade and that if it would amuse me there was a vacant seat in his bedroom which overlooked the village green. There had been a frost in the night and it was a pleasure to stretch one's limbs on hard roads in the keen crisp air after the winter's confinement in trenches. Hill was on parade with his battalion and we were received by Keys, his servant, who brought chairs and cigarettes and Hill's field-glasses, but they were not necessary; from that second floor window we could see everything. The men were already drawn up in a great square, inside which a single line of duck boards had been laid in order that the General could walk round without stepping in the mud. At the far end of the green where he was expected to arrive, a flagstaff had been erected, and from it the Tricolor hung limply in the still air. Keys told us in his dry way about the fatigue parties from this resting Brigade that had been at work for days on these preparations, about the hours spent in spit and polish, and the numerous rehearsals. He said the men had been there already for a good hour. For a long time nothing happened, then the band broke into the "Marseillaise"; we looked everywhere for the great man but he was nowhere to be seen. It was only another rehearsal. We waited once more. A pompous, thick-set fellow with a long row of ribbons across his chest took the stage; he was the Regimental Sergeant-Major. There was a lot of closing in and more shuffling as he checked the dressing of the Middlesex rank by rank. The movement was repeated in the next battalion and suddenly Keys pointed to a corner of the green where a string of cars had pulled up.

General Nivelle descended from the first car. The band rather hurriedly struck up the "Marseillaise", the troops presented arms, and for a moment the Commander-in-Chief stood very still with his hand at the salute. Immediately the music ceased he began to walk rapidly round the square. He did not leave the duck-boards, he appeared to be in great haste and hardly noticed the men, stopping only to shake hands with the Colonels of the battalions. He hurried on, followed by a string of staff officers, mostly British, who filed after him keeping to the boards. Immediately he had shaken hands with the last Colonel the "Marseillaise" again broke out, as if the bandmaster were fearful that the General might escape before he had worked off his orders. The Commander-in-Chief stood till it was finished and remained at the salute while the band played the English National Anthem; then he entered his car and the Staff got into theirs. The inspection was over before anyone realised it had really begun.

Keys thought that there was another inspection of a battery somewhere on the outskirts of the village, but he was not certain—and besides we did not care. A sense of irritation was left by this perfunctory inspection. There was a feeling that the men had been fooled. Yet it was absurd to fall out of temper on such a day; the crisp, clean air got into one's blood, and as I went along the high road that took me back to Fouquières, I found myself walking faster and faster. I wanted to run and shout and slap someone on the back, to do something, to start off somewhere. The inspection was forgotten, for all generals were a joke. Life itself was a joke.

In a field on the outskirts of the village a sergeant was putting some of the last draft through squad drill. I paused and watched through the hedge. The fellow seemed to take a strange delight in making some wretched man look foolish before the others. He gave an order, then yelled "As you were," stopping to pour on the head of the culprit a stream of invective and of sarcasm. But the men were not as amused as they were meant to be. Clearly they had no use for this bully. Now that he had seen me his energy was redoubled. Standing there I began to feel uncomfortable, as if I were in league with the fellow. I walked on and came to an outhouse near the château which had been cleared and converted into baths for the brigade. The place was full of steam; it rose from everything, from the great tubs of water, from the floor, from the walls and bodies of the bathers. Out of the steam came shouts and sounds of splashing water and their absurd songs. A man bent to lift a footboard that hid a bit of soap perhaps, or a wandering stud; his dark wet hair hung over his eyes like a fringe. He seized a towel and as he plied it with both hands in a sawing movement the muscles of his back where it broadened into the great shoulders rippled beneath the skin which glowed pink as a child's.

"Everything all right?" I asked.

"Yes, sir," they answered in chorus with immense gusto. They were like great children, these fellows, and I stood watching them for a long time.

It has been a bad winter in the trenches and these cottages seem very homely and attractive with their fires, their beds and kindly people. In the afternoon I often find my way to the little house that is my billet, where madame and the children and I will talk for hours. But on this particular day I did not want to talk. For a long time I sat staring into the fire, which flickered and crumbled to ash. Gradually my thoughts became less bitter and lost their edges, and soon ceased to be thoughts at all. I seemed to be floating in air, though I heard still as in a dream the ticking of the old clock; it beat drowsily to and fro, grew fainter. Slowly, imperceptibly, sleep fell like a curtain between me and the confusion of the world.

When I awoke it was dark and the fire had gone out. I got up feeling cold and stiff and went out into the street. All the estaminets were full of men; they were attracted like moths by the blaze of light in the windows, or perhaps by the noise of singing. Out of a corner house a man came and through the open door the sound of voices suddenly became louder. When the door closed with a bang it died down abruptly, and grew fainter and fainter as I moved away. Now that I was clear of the village not a sound broke the hush that had fallen on everything. Aimlessly I wandered up dark lanes and back through the deserted streets. A curious feeling of loneliness and depression crept over me as the events of the day moved through my head.

First the naïve anticipation among the troops; these men of the 73rd Brigade were rather looking forward to an international inspection. Though they were frankly a little disappointed that it was not Joffre, this Nivelle must, they supposed, be the leading French General. He was no doubt curious to see English Infantry for himself, and they were quite convinced that the 73rd had been picked out of our huge army to represent British troops on account of their good work on the Somme. Then the show had begun. It became plain that this Frenchman was not thinking of them at all. For him there were no individual units—just troops, numbers, a force in being, a figure on paper. We could see he was impatient to get away to the conference that had brought him into those parts. He seemed to grudge these few minutes wasted on a ceremonial parade which could do no good and was to him only a tiresome part of international diplomacy necessary when two nations take the field as allies. Then the drill scene came back to me, the licking into shape of the last draft by the Prussian sergeant. And then the baths; the animals must be sent to market in good fettle. Finally the men, left to themselves, had sought out the estaminets where for a space they could forget.

It was plain from that day's events that the Division was

C

being fattened for the fight. I hurried on as if these doubts could be sweated out like a fever but they stuck. That habit of questioning things that had come over me of late would not be put away. The war was no longer the straight issue it had once been. I was no longer sure of anything. In a battle somehow the horror of this business of war is not felt. Nature has the stop on; perhaps we are half doped to come through it at all. But when you get into Divisional rest, right back here under peace conditions, when you see the men full of life and fun, it is then that the stupid cruelty of the things eats into the mind. There is talk in the newspapers of a kind of crusade, of the impatience of the men burning to get at the Hun, of troops in a battle unwilling to be relieved. And perhaps these things happen. But there is nothing about those who find they are not equipped for the business, who falter and hang back. They are pushed back into the line and in their tale there is no room for rhetoric. We are all changing out here and things happen that set us thinking.

One day when we were in the trenches a man reported sick and I sent him back to duty. The following day he came again and again I sent him back. But the day after he was still there among the morning sick. "It's no good sir," he said, "I can't stick it no longer." Once more I thoroughly overhauled him; there was nothing wrong with him physically and he was sane enough. He was simply tired—but so were others. Once more I sent him back. Next day he was killed.

A friendly critic has expressed a fear that the soldier who has not been seasoned by battle may be discouraged by all this fulminating against the iniquity of war. The idea is to hide from him what war is really like until he finds it out for himself. It would be as reasonable to keep the medical student away from disease because some may become a little too introspective and get it into their heads that they themselves are suffering from the same malady. I have already warned the reader that this book is a record of changing moods; sometimes fresh from some more personal loss I have written as though I were a pacifist and war was sheer waste, sometimes it is plain that I held war to be the ultimate test of manhood. Besides, I will not tamper with the testimony it carries, however badly it may have worn with time. It is well that those who command men in war—and it is for them I write—should have known such moods, if they recognise them for what they are, that they may the better detect them in others. The imaginative man in war pays a price which is not exacted from his more stolid brother, but his men are the more ready to follow his example when they divine that he has read their secret thoughts.

WAR WITH FATE

Before I had ever been under fire I was walking up the Lille road from Armentières after the light had gone when the Boche turned a machine gun on to the road; my companion subsided into a ditch before I realised what was happening. At Ypres six months later walking behind him along a path that was being shelled I could not detect a tremor; he might have been on parade.

A man may duck his head when a bullet pings past his ear because he has not learnt to take charge of himself. I can remember the cold douche to my self-respect when first I found myself at the mercy of my instincts. But these antics are not in our control; it is too late to try to suppress them when at a stroke they take us by surprise. Only by the birth of a proper attitude to danger can we hope to discipline the frailty of the flesh. Ducking comes from a morbid alertness. The poor fellow is obsessed with a desire to come through. It does not happen when all alternatives have been put away. At Ypres my friend had won his secret battle with fear, he no longer thought of an alternative.

A form of fatalism was common especially in the ranks. There was a runner attached to Headquarters, a tight-lipped, silent fellow who when he was told that he could go on leave replied he did not want to go, he had no friends. He was always taking messages up unhealthy roads out of his turn. One day, while he accompanied me to the trenches, I spoke of a man in "A" Company who was not wearing well. "It ain't no use, sir, if you're for it, you're for it." I looked at him quickly, being windy myself at that time, but if he had suspected me he would have said nothing. Time had stilled his suspicion of me as a mere civilian. Presently the Boche turned a machine gun on the road. I had the liveliest desire to step into the ditch but was checked by the presence of this fellow at my elbow. After that I was not much bothered. Perhaps too I came to think with Tolstoy that every bullet has a billet. "We are all fatalists now," I wrote about that time. But was the renunciation complete?

From time to time the desire to live surged up in our hearts. At Ypres in 1915 I left the trenches with Weston to make our way to Poperinghe where the leave train would meander through the night to Boulogne. Our horses had been brought to the Asylum on the outskirts of Ypres. Ambling along we saw presently occasional shells falling on a village through which we must pass. We found ourselves standing in the middle of the road gazing at the familiar sight, then without a word and as if the horses had taken charge we took to the fields. When at last we pulled up our steaming horses we had made a wide détour; so completely had the desire to come through with leave at hand damped down our sense of humour; into our minds had crept an alternative.

The appetite for life was not confined to those about to go on leave.

"For God's sake, Johnson, can't you talk about something besides the bloody war," Tommy said, and rushed out of the mess. I have recorded that remark elsewhere in this book as a sign of wear and tear, but apart from that, an underlying, perhaps half-conscious resentment against fate was common among the boys who came to us as subalterns. It was bad enough that month after month should pass in that sort of existence among older officers, who were always talking of the good time they had had before the war when these lads were at school. But soon they began to suspect that this dreary life was the only kind of existence most of them would ever know. And as time went on it was not only these boys who felt they were at war with fate. Many officers on leave came to think they were entitled to a degree of licence they had not dreamt of taking before they went to France. This was their last chance to get something out of life while it lasted; if they had been cast by fate for this lousy part in the trenches they would at least do what they liked while they could; another leave was a gamble. Of course they did not reason it out in that fashion, most men just relaxed the discipline of their own lives.

The idea that we could do as we liked during the few days we were allowed in England led me to break all the conventions of my upbringing by calling on a man whom I did not know on a pretext which I should have deemed flimsy and even absurd had I been in a normal mood. It was done, I think, on the impulse of the moment on the last day of my leave. I had discovered from the telephone directory that Mr. Edmund Gosse lived in Regent's Park. When I rang the bell and asked if Mr. Gosse was at home the maid without more ado conducted me to a conservatory where he greeted me myopically, gazing expectantly through his spectacles. I do not recall any feeling of embarrassment. I told him without delay that I proposed to write a book on the war and had come there to ask his advice. Mr. Gosse answered that if I had anything to say I ought to say it plainly, that it must not be a fake, by which I believe he meant a novel. For half an hour he developed this theme, which I think interested him, but I have long forgotten what he said. When he had done, his voice became kindly, he hesitated. "I trust you are not going back to France," he said. Mr. Gosse in his books was always busy with aspects and impressions, but on this occasion he displayed no curiosity as to what was happening in France, nor in anything that I might have to tell him of a clash on such a scale between passionate men.

IN WHICH WAR APPEARS RIDICULOUS

How it began I never knew. The water in the trenches had risen day after day till life at last was no longer endurable. Anyway, for the officers in the companies, the Christmas truce of 1914 just happened. But when it was all fixed up I think I can guess who were the first to leave the trenches. Then, when no shot was fired, I can see others join them, and later some Boche cautiously appearing from his trench. The war had simply fizzled out. We found the men strolling behind the trenches, while but a hundred yards away the Saxons were hard at work with pick and spade; a few of the more venturesome met in the middle of no-man's-land and passed the time of day, since these Saxons spoke English without much difficulty. It made war appear unreal, for they seemed very much like anybody else, kindly folk, many of them students from Leipzic, who plainly bore us no ill-will. We were even allowed to gather that no love was lost between them and the Prussians. Some dead cows lay between the lines, with here and there a horse, swollen and bloated, its legs jutting stiffly into space like an overturned wooden horse.

For days no shot was fired. Through the short hours of daylight both sides worked on the top, and when night fell not a sound came across the misty fields; men came and went at all times as if they were in England. The Saxons and our people alike were bent that no act of theirs should reflect on the honour of their truce, and when one day a spare from far over on the right hit one of our men as he wandered overland, they were quick to explain—it was the Prussians, they said. And they had arranged that three volleys fired high in rapid succession should end the truce. The men of course were like children; they dearly loved a new game; they were glad to get out of the water for a little and to stretch their stiff limbs.

The Boche appeared to have no difficulty in getting material; our men worked too, some dug and some prepared wattle hurdles for revetting, but soon it was plain that he would be ready before our job was half finished. Then, when his men could live above ground, behind their breastworks, the truce must end, his officers would see to that. And so it happened. One day about noon as the men were digging, three volleys were fired high above our heads. A big brown fellow beside me stopped, he looked up at the German trench, grinned, and began to dig again. Now the men were getting into the trench, sauntering back talking and laughing. After a time he too shouldered his spade and slowly made towards the trench, for it was clear that the truce had ended as it began, suddenly and for no apparent reason.

That war might be unpleasant, uncomfortable, sometimes even terrible, had always appeared possible, that it should seem ridiculous—that was new. It had always been strange that the mass of people who will believe in anything should be at the mercy of the few who believe in nothing. Suddenly I had asked myself if the war was necessary. That attitude to war had been forced upon us for a short space; it appeared to vanish when we got back into our trenches.

Some who kept that truce have gone into middle-age, and that which seemed no more than a passing fancy has become, after a quarter of a century, the deep-rooted faith of our sons, the youth of England. War settles nothing, they say. And now when they have been driven to arms by Hitler, we shall do well to mark that they have not gone as we went to the high adventure of 1914, with our hearts singing. They will remember.

A PLEA FOR CHIVALRY

The English are not good haters. During the thirty months I was with the 1st Royal Fusiliers I cannot recall a single man who lost his temper with the enemy. So it is not easy for us to understand Ludendorff's saying that the emotion of hate is a power which ought to be made use of in time of war. Trotter finds the explanation of this instinctive difference between the English and the Germans in the tendency of gregarious animals to develop into various types. Members of the wolf-pack derive encouragement from hearing the rest of the pack giving tongue; it preserves contact, and it stimulates in each the due degree of aggressive rage. "This serious and narrow passion", he says, "tends naturally to concentrate itself upon some external object or quarry, which becomes by that fact an object of hate, to the exclusion of any other feeling, whether of sympathy, self-possession or a sense of the ludicrous." The curious spectacle of Germans greeting one another with "Gott strafe England" was a manifestation of an instinctive necessity. Their war-cries and war-songs met a want in the German's nature to which he ministered with a grave fervour. The English Tommy found them great fun; "Gott strafe Tickler" he shouted back. And when the Hymn of Hate drifted over from the German line he would compete with gusto with Fritz' rendering of that strange product of patriotism. The failure of the English army to take such war-cries and war-songs seriously does not mean that as a race we are less subject to the tyranny of instinct than the Teuton, but only that in a people of the socialized type, such as the English, unity depends on a different kind of bond, and our morale does not rest upon the narrow intensities of aggressive rage. Even in the winter of 1917 when we no longer believed in anything we never grew bitter.

For many months men have watched this heartbreaking muddle with its waste of life. They could not help noticing it and talked about it a good deal. But in the end they always found the word in extenuation. They argued that this man meant well or in the final resort that he was a trier. Everyone was the same in this, men were taken on the Staff because they were liked and if a General was relieved of his command another post was immediately found for him. At first this had worried me, too often I saw the results on stretchers. Now I have come to see that this immense toleration is just English. It is not found among dominion troops, it is not Irish nor Scotch but only English. That is where we differ from the Prussians, we are tolerant of everything. And this attitude is impossible where there exists a relentless demand for efficiency, it is no part of the creed of men for whom success in life is everything. If it had been otherwise, if we had weeded out inefficiency without mercy or remorse, and put the struggle on a clean, hard business footing, the war might now be over, but we should have had to change our character to win. Toleration was as far as we had got towards a religion: to live and let live, and then nothing in the war seemed to matter if we came out at the end with this spirit. Surely if men stripped of their illusions can endure without bitterness so many and so great privations, then this game is worth the candle.

Even now after a quarter of a century I can recall the occasion when a little fissure appeared first in the unbroken front of unquestioning acceptance which I in common with the Youth of 1914 presented to war. It was at Armentières

in May, 1915, when two patrols met in the darkness just
beyond our wire. There were shots, then the Boche took to
their heels, but one big fellow showed fight. A little later
they dragged him into the trench, and stripped the buttons
and shoulder straps from his tunic, and turned out his
pockets that his unit might be known, and left him for
dead.

Next morning before dawn when they came to bury him
in a ditch behind the line, he was breathing still, but when
they brought him into the dressing-station he was dead.
The men dumped him in an outhouse of the farm full of
litter and every kind of refuse. His shirt was open at his
great bull neck, showing his hairy chest, his Hun skull was
flattened behind and covered all over with a stiff stubble,
his feet were tied together with a bit of bandage, leaving
the nailed soles of his enormous boots facing you in the
doorway. Surely that immense fellow existed only in cari-
cature. All that day men of the company in reserve came
and gaped through the open door at the dead Boche, and
some went in and cut souvenirs from what was left of his
clothing. Towards evening the adjutant passing that way
saw what was afoot and ordered a sergeant to place a guard
upon the door.

About the same hour, when the light had nearly gone, a
man who had been sniped that day was brought from the
trenches for burial. He was borne on a stretcher to the
corner of the French cemetery assigned to the British, where
the small wooden crosses in their neat rows contrasted
strangely with the ornate monuments of the citizens of
Armentières that jostled each other for space in the rest of
the graveyard. One of the men furtively removed his cap,
then another, until they stood bareheaded around the grave,
looking at their feet, muffling their movements. Save when
a spent bullet struck the stone slabs, or a few spares whined
high over our heads, there was no sound now but the voice
of the Padre rising and falling like the suck of the tide.

When it was over the men hung about a little in twos and threes; they did not speak, and began presently to melt away, until there were three of us alone in the cemetery in the gloom of the night. Then the adjutant spoke to the drum-major; they left the cemetery and went out into a field beyond, where a grave had been dug; the drum-major began reluctantly to read a few sentences over the dead German, fumbling with the prayer-book by the light of a torch. When he had done, the adjutant ordered him to tell off two men under a corporal to fill in the grave.

From the road the farm rose up out of the night, only a little darker than the rest; a grey cat slunk away noiselessly, its belly brushing the ground. In the stillness that had fallen on everything there was a sound of footsteps coming up the road, and out of the darkness a man's voice, "Anyway, mate, that's one bloody Hun less."

War is said to expose the savage that lurks in men. It excites, we are told, those ugly primitive passions which civilisation had decently interred. It may be so—yet I have seen more cold cruelty in a month of the competitive life of London in peace than came my way in more than two years with a battalion in war. That this poor devil should be put away like that, outside the pale, because he had more heart than his fellows, was something new; the gassing at Ypres had altered everything. The old Army was a small family-affair, and when in April, 1915, tales began to drift down from the Ypres Salient of gassed men fighting for their breath, who had crawled on all fours out of the battle, those simple folk were moved to anger. The war was not going to be as clean.

Yet this incident of the German patrol stands in a place apart in my diary, the solitary expression of feeling on the part of the men against the enemy. Soon it was forgotten; men spoke again of "Fritz" with amusement and tolerance. They had nothing against him; they followed the same craft; he was only doing his job just as they were. With me too that mood quickly passed, many months went by before doubt and uncertainty found a way into my head, but it seems to me now that this Boche corporal was the first to lay hands on my peace of mind.

I have told this story because I believe this hate business belongs to the shape of things that are gone. It has been the big blunderbuss in the armoury of those in authority, to be fired off whenever they wished to stiffen the people against the enemy. Does it help even for a day to liken the Germans to vermin which must be destroyed? If I may speak for those now in the army, half the propaganda spewed about is useless stuff; it defeats its own purpose. For the youth of to-day, unless his credulity has been persistently exploited, as in Germany, gets no sense of adventure as we did in 1914 from setting off to the wars. For him it is a senseless piece of folly that solves nothing; if he goes to fight it is only a distasteful duty to be got through as quickly as may be. If he is going to be fed on this hate stuff, his disgust with the whole iniquitous affair may fulminate into something beyond our reckoning. He is more squeamish than we were; he has no stomach for the hot fury of passionate men in what is to him a cold-blooded if inevitable task, like tackling a mad dog that it may do no hurt to others.

I want to tell another tale because it speaks of the only mood in which men are ready to see this war through. Moreover, those whom I left in France would have been quick to post up what counted to the credit of the enemy. I had written in my diary "Of one who liked war", the phrase had a strange sound even then, now it seems hardly credible.

At Bayenhem, when the Division was resting, Hill told me casually that Gordon, an officer in "D" Company was kicking his heels to get back to the line. Most of us were quite content to do nothing; we were in no hurry to go back to the mud and monotony of the trenches, and I wanted to know if Gordon's restlessness was genuine, why he preferred the trenches to that peaceful existence in a village that might have been in England. I questioned Hill, but he was not very helpful. He told me that Gordon was in his College Boat at Oxford; he seemed to have an idea at the back of his mind that he had not yet pulled his weight, though already in the war he had been severely wounded in the neck. Bow had done this, and Four that, and now the crew was down to three. He had an obsession about this boat; he was secretly bent on bringing some credit to it. Gordon was not an easy man to get to know, but when I saw more of him I was satisfied that this was the real aggressive spirit, so strange to most of us who had been out for some time and never went out of our way to look for trouble. There it was beneath the stolid exterior, covered up by all the negatives the average young Briton of his type thinks valuable.

One day after our return to the salient while he was at the transport, his company was rather heavily shelled. When he returned and learnt what had happened he said nothing, but seemed put out; Hill thought he was brooding on it. Then one night, without a word to anyone, he went out on patrol taking a corporal with him. He did not come back. He had gone in his leather waistcoat, without a coat or anything that might give away his unit if he were captured. He had emptied his pockets of letters and papers. People said to go off like that without telling anyone was a silly thing to do, but that he was a good fellow and would be a loss. Months later a communication came from Germany through the American Red Cross. I print it because it gave me new heart at a time when I was less certain of things.

On the morning of the 24th January on the Ypern front, near four big holes caused by the bursting of shells, north-west of the Bellevarde Farm, and about 30 metres distant from the German front measuring from the west to the east, an Englishman was buried, a German officer in charge. The body had lain for a fortnight or three weeks before our front (here followed a full description with minute details about studs and underclothing). The wounds consisted of a shot in the heart so that death was instantaneous. Since the burial was carried out by the young officer in charge, although at great personal risk as he was under fire at the time, and since his only object was to give his enemy an honourable burial, in the hope that this action would be of some comfort to the relatives of the dead man, I beg that this description may be sent to the English troops on the Ypern front.

Mark that minute description of the clothing, though Gordon was buried in no man's land after dark. Mark those comfortable words "The wounds consisted of a shot in the heart, so that death was instantaneous." I am glad to think that Gordon was decently buried by a gallant enemy. This was a man without fear who had brought from Oxford the young clean zest of his kind into the mixed business of war. Providence did well to revive the ancient chivalry of arms for his going out.

In my account of these incidents written as they happened I have tried to depict the mood that was their aftermath. But I can now measure more accurately how far these moods represented a stretching of my moral fibre, though I still cannot tell to what extent war with fate, the resentment of an individual against fate which had marked him down for annihilation, contributed to his defeat. But the feeling left by the Christmas truce of 1914 that war was unnecessary hardly broke the skin. And my disgust with the treatment of the wounded Boche corporal was only a passing mood of discouragement, as fleeting apparently as the heartening effect of German chivalry which I have recorded in the description of Gordon's death. I say "apparently" for I am not sure that anything which makes a soldier doubt whether the game is worth the candle can be set aside so lightly. As long as he feels there is only one thing to do he will do it. If he begins to think of an alternative then his purpose falters. But the revolt that grew in my heart against this killing business—the constant fret of casualties—was another story. The battalion kept changing, seven Colonels came and went and I could never school myself to grow indifferent to these gaps. They left wounds which even now are hardly healed and my own decline in morale in the last months of the winter of 1916-17—obvious enough to me though not, I think, to others—was probably the outcome of those wounds.

Chapter Five

How courage is spent

Courage is a moral quality; it is not a chance gift of nature like an aptitude for games. It is a cold choice between two alternatives, the fixed resolve not to quit; an act of renunciation which must be made not once but many times by the power of the will. Courage is will power.

The story of how courage was spent in France is a picture of sensitive men using up their will power under discouraging circumstances while one by one their moral props were knocked down. The call on the bank might be only the daily drain of the trenches, or it might be a sudden draft which threatened to close the account. The acid test of a man in the trenches was high explosive; it told each one of us things about ourselves we had not known till then.

One summer day in 1916, the Boche put over a few shells. We did not stop what we were doing or worry about them; it had happened before without doing much harm, but when the shelling became heavier we got down to the bottom of the trench waiting, listening. We heard a shell that seemed by its rising shriek to be coming near. Then there was a shattering noise, in our ears it seemed, a cloud of

61

fumes and a great shower of earth and blood and human remains. As the fumes drifted away I had just time to notice that the man on my right had disappeared and that the trench where he had stood was now only a mound of freshly turned earth, when another angry shriek ended in another rending explosion, and more fumes enveloped us. Our bit of the trench was isolated now and as the shells burst all around with gathering violence it seemed that the whole of the Boche artillery was watching this little island and was intent on its destruction. At first I thought of what was happening to others near me, but soon I did not even think of what might happen to myself. My mind became a complete blank. I had a feeling as if I had suffered physical hurt though I was not touched, the will to do the right thing was for the moment stunned. I could not think at all. I was dazed and at the mercy of those beckoning instincts which till then I had been able to fight. Perhaps I should have got up and run if my limbs had seemed to belong to me. And at the end there was peace again and a strange quietness and the old queer feeling of satisfaction after a bad time as if something had been achieved, then utter weariness, a desire to sleep, a numb feeling.

The war had never been the same since, something in the will had snapped. In a good battalion a shaken company soon recovers but it is different, the life of the men in it as fighting soldiers has been abbreviated as a severe illness that is seemingly thrown off may in the end shorten a man's life. That sort of thing did not come often. Many who were months in the trenches escaped it altogether. Even in the Somme, in our little part of it, though there was plenty of shelling there was time in between the shelling to pull oneself together. It was when the Boche was out to obliterate a trench, when the shells came over in one continuous stream that the true test came. It was my only experience of the real thing in more than two years with the battalion. But once it had happened it was always there, and every shell that fell near the trench seemed to be but the beginning of a new cataclysm. At the time I do not think I was much frightened, I was too stunned to think. But it took its toll later. I was to go through it many times in my sleep and then the mind was no longer doped, it hurt. Even when the war had begun to fade out of men's minds I used to hear all at once without warning the sound of a shell coming. Perhaps it was only the wind in the trees to remind me that war had exacted its tribute and that my little capital was less than it had been.

There were men in France who were ready to go out but who could not meet death in that shape. They were prepared for it if it came swiftly and cleanly. But that shattering, crude bloody end by a big shell was too much for them. It was something more than death, all their plans for meeting it with decency and credit were suddenly battered down; it was not so much that their lives were in danger as that their self-respect had gone out of their hands. They were at the crisis of their lives dishevelled, plastered with mud and earth and blood; their actions at the mercy of others, they were no longer certain what they might do. That dread experience was the last stone of the house of fear built out of all those instincts that were drawing men away from danger back to security and the ways of peace. It had frightened more men away from the trenches than anything else; a man who passed that test and was still a man had nothing more to fear from life.

One of my students, Lovelock, used to say that once and only once in a season could he summon the will power to race all out. He was thinking of the supreme crisis of an Olympic struggle with the world to beat. He meant that he could not call too often on his reserves of nervous energy. Even prodigal youth had to husband its resources. Likewise in the trenches a man's will power was his capital and he was always spending, so that wise and thrifty company officers watched the expenditure of every penny lest their

men went bankrupt. When their capital was done, they
were finished.

Mr. Duff Cooper in his life of Lord Haig has put forward
as an axiom another conception of courage:

> The British army was a citizen army only half-
> trained to war. The survivors (of the Somme) in mid-
> November were veterans. The British were taught to
> fight.

This may be allowed: if a soldier is always using up his
capital he may from time to time add to it. There is a paying in as well as a paying out. When General Alexander
took over the command in the Western Desert the men as
often as not did not bother to salute an officer, but after the
battle of El Alamein all that came to an end. Their self
respect came back, for achievement is a sharp tonic to
morale. Again loyalty to a fine battalion may take hold of a
man and stiffen his purpose; the confidence of the tried
soldier replaces the old vague fear of the unknown. But in
the main time is against the soldier. "The British were
taught to fight." That was not the lesson the Somme taught
me. The day the battalion was taken out of the battle I
wrote:

> All around me are the faces of men who do not seem
> to have slept for a week. Some who were tired before
> look ill; the very gait of the men has lost its spring. The
> sap has gone out of them. They are dried up.

Men wear out in war like clothes. When Mr. Duff Cooper
writes that the Army was taught to fight by the Somme, he
is preaching from the text of his master which changed the
character of the war after the first battle of Ypres. That
doctrine grew out of the fanatical sense of duty of a Scotch
covenanter unversed in the workings of the human mind.

The Army was to be blooded in a hundred raids, a hundred limited offensives, as the only way to preserve, or was it to create, the offensive spirit. It was to dissipate like a spend-thrift not only the lives but the moral heritage of the youth of England.

Chapter Six

Nemesis of deception

The winter of 1916-17 was a time of doubt and disillusionment. Men were weary, less certain of things. There was a feeling abroad that it was necessary to believe in someone or something to carry on at all. It had not been easy. The garbled accounts of the correspondents in France had done incalculable harm. Men, knowing the facts, rose up against that fancy literature. "You can't believe a thing you read," they said. The success of trench raids was no longer measured by statements of dug-outs blown up and Huns destroyed; only prisoners counted; no journalism could bring in prisoners.

First Army Intelligence No. 724 First Army Front. The enemy attempted a raid on our line near the Loos Crassier at 6 a.m. this morning. After severe fighting he was driven off, several dead Germans being left close to our parapet and wire; two of these have since been brought in and their identifications shew them to have belonged to the 153rd Regiment, 8th Division, 4th Corps. This shows no change in the distribution of the German forces opposite the Loos salient except that the position of the 153rd Regiment is slightly further South than had hitherto been supposed.

Lt. Col. General Staff,
First Army.

Friday, January 5th, 1917.

We were told how the enemy attempting a raid on our line after severe fighting only succeeded in leaving identifications behind, which confirmed the disposition of the 153rd Regiment as elucidated by our Intelligence Department. Next day the public were told this in *The Times* under two big black headlines:

Times. January 6th.

German Raiders near Loos
Heavy trench fighting

The following telegraphic dispatch was received yesterday from G.H.Q. in France, 8.36 p.m. Early this morning a hostile raiding party succeeded in entering our trenches south of Loos. Heavy fighting ensued and the enemy was speedily driven out, leaving a number of dead in our trenches. Some of our men are missing—

Readers of *The Times* would scarcely deduce from this that the Boche stayed forty minutes in our trenches extracting fifty-one prisoners from the deep dug-outs in the support line of the battalion on our right, that a corporal and two men stuck to a machine gun otherwise there was little fight shown, and that subsequently after a court of enquiry the officer commanding this battalion was removed from his command. This little incident is such a perfect specimen of its kind that Charles Montagu lifted it bodily from a letter I had written to *The Times* and dumped it in his *Disenchantment* in a chapter on the "Duty of Lying".

The censor may have to draw his blue pencil through the truth for more reasons than one. Those who are compelled to be spectators might take hardly the tale of what actually happens in war. Stories like Loos are only tolerable because the same thing might befall the listener at any time. It made all the difference when a man could not share the fruits of incompetence.

However that may be, the cooking of news before it was served up to the public in England was a prime factor in unsettling opinion in France. Men could not help seeing that this news was altered not because it gave information to the enemy for he already knew it; they were left to speculate in whose interests such editing was carried out. The repeated appearance of the old Adam among their leaders had taken the heart out of people in France. Bad enough to find—and they often did—that the mental outfit for leadership was wanting, but what of this cynicism at the top? Had nothing changed? Men began to ask themselves in dumb dismay what was the good of it all. Authority declined, scepticism grew apace, men became critical.

When I think of that sceptical attitude of 1917, I think too of the easy acceptance of the spring of 1915 when we were told that there were only a few weary German divisions between us and Lille. If that was meant to hearten the men of the old army it displayed a grotesque ignorance of the material then available. But it was not so meant, and I have kept a little printed pamphlet with a blue cover which was issued to us at Armentières before the battle of Neuve Chapelle, containing a list of towns and villages, including Lille and far beyond, with neat notes on the taps, pumps and other sources of drinking water. The events of those two years of war had slowly eaten away my faith in the infallibility of authority; for me that began with that little blue book with its unfulfilled hopes.

Chapter Seven

No rest, no moment's peace

High explosive put fear in a new frame. But the essence of it lay in this, that it happened to passive men. Since the discovery of firearms, science has been pushing armies apart, and as long ago as the war with Napoleon, a surgeon with Wellington's army in Spain found hardly any bayonet wounds. Hand to hand fighting is vanishing out of war, and even veterans have never met cold steel, which was the way death came to the ancients. Once when I had a bayonet a few inches from my belly I was more frightened than by any shell, but it left nothing behind it. It went out of my mind, it would never happen again.

Fear takes new shapes, but it used to come upon men suddenly and was gone. The real difference between the war of 1914 and the wars of history lay in the absence of a close period, when men safe for the moment could rest and build up a reserve. It ended inevitably in the breaking of men who would have passed the test of any single day's fighting with credit; many too were broken for good, they could not come again. There was no rest, no moment's peace. Now and then that was driven home. The Medical Officer of the Durhams, a decent little fellow, who had come through the Hooge show in August, 1915, without a scratch, was standing in the woods before Poperinghe, miles from the line, enjoying the quiet peace of the summer evening when his head was taken off by a stray shell. That was the only shell, as far as I can remember which dropped in those woods in our time. It was not cricket.

There was a fellow, too, in the Regiment, the last of four brothers, all serving soldiers, who had been found a safe job as batman to the transport officer. It was felt his family had done its bit, and everyone wanted him to come through. When his master went on leave he was attached for the time to headquarters to do odd jobs and to make himself useful. One morning he had hardly left the hut after bringing me water when there was a sound like a whizz-bang, only you could hear it coming before it burst, and then a shower of earth spattered against the hut. I looked out. The fellow had been caught by a direct hit, and above, high up, a droning sound grew fainter. It was the first time we had been bombed, one little solitary bomb, away back there near Poperinghe; it could not be chance, the men said.

Those two fatalities made a bigger dint in my mind than anything which had happened in the trenches. By day or by night, in trenches or in billets, whatever the odds, still there was no such thing as one moment's complete security. So, as the war dragged on, as the wear and tear of the trench life told, we came to think less of the gaudy act performed on the spur of the moment, to value more the worth of the man who was prepared to see the thing through.

This man was often hard pressed and the healing effect of leave sometimes kept him on his feet. If the soldier can look forward to leave, his spirits rise—he has hope in his heart and hope is the best preservative in war—in Gaelic hope and courage are the same word. The Germans know the necessity of a break. In the summer of 1940 after the Western offensive against France forty divisions were sent to Germany. Even in the first war a few veterans who had

survived a long period of trench warfare were given a
month's leave, and now, in this war, there is a limit to the
demands made on flying officers. In the Bomber Command,
after twenty-five or thirty sorties over enemy territory, the
pilot is given six months rest. There is a point on the horizon, something to hope for.

To fix such a point and to order a pilot to be rested at
that moment, whatever his own desire, has not won general
acceptance. There are two schools of thought. Some senior
officers affirm that if there is no limit to the demands we
make on a pilot, an attitude of fatalism will grow up. This
is a brief phase. Presently he becomes reckless, then things
happen. Other officers of no less experience are sceptical of
attempts to patch up men who are cracking. They question
whether a pilot who is wearing badly will fly again. They
complain that of those who have been given rest, few return
to their flying duties: perhaps they have married or become
part of the ground staff or would lose promotion by their
return. Certainly if a pilot does not fly, he quickly loses his
form. He begins to think of a ground job, of how good life
is. Into his mind an alternative has crept, and when an
officer looks over his shoulder the chance of a safe berth
will come sooner or later.

The question at issue is of some consequence in war. If a
man is rested in time will he have another summer of high
achievement, or if that is only a forlorn hope is it more
sensible to cut losses? To put it differently, can a good fellow who is showing signs of wear and tear come back? A
senior officer at the headquarters of Bomber Command told
me this tale: he knew a pilot in the last war who had a good
record but presently began to return from a flight before
the others; something always went wrong with his engine,
or some other part of his craft. He was warned that if it
happened again he would lose his commission and be sent
to England. But a week later once more he came back,
blaming his machine. The fellow was sent home and no

more was heard of him for a time. Then he wrote that joining the Royal Fusiliers as a private, he had been promoted sergeant and had been awarded the Distinguished Conduct Medal.

Air Commodore Symonds writes:

> A fighter pilot who had previously flown light bombers in the Battle of France said that during this time he hardly ever saw targets or the effect of his bombs. After a while he sweated every time he got into an aeroplane he was so frightened; he could not sleep. Later in a Hurricane in the Battle of Britain he found (those are his own words) "Success in the game is the great incentive to subdue fear. Once you've shot down two or three the effect is terrific and you'll go on till you're killed. It's love of the sport rather than sense of duty that makes you go on without minding how much you are shot up." This young officer was severely wounded in combat but was flying his Hurricane again within one month and went on to destroy many enemy aircraft, win several decorations and command his Squadron.

It is no part of my business to spread a gloss over the motives of the pilot in his Hurricane. The idea that is greater than fear which fortifies men in facing danger is never quite the same. Very different emotions may steel men to superlative bravery, in some there is a selfless dedication to the task in hand, in others the driving force may even jar a little on our sense of the fitness of things.

Here is another pilot who came back. Let Symonds, a close observer, tell the tale.

> This was an officer, aged twenty-five. Although he was in general high spirited and adventurous he volunteered that as a child he had always what he called a strong safety factor. He swam, but he didn't dive. At eighteen he entered the Air Force. He wanted

to fly. He did well. He thought his safety factor helped him. He never took undue risks. In 1939 he was lost in a snow-storm for two hours and coming to the end of his petrol made a forced landing in hilly country with no visibility. It was a fortunate escape. For two days after this he felt shaken. "I couldn't believe I had got away with it: I had to touch things to make sure of their reality." He then started flying again. He had completed over 1,000 hours flying before the war and in virtue of his good flying obtained accelerated promotion. After the outbreak of war, early in his operational career he was second pilot in a twin-engined bomber off the Norwegian coast when an engine failed. During the next twenty-five minutes he organised the crew to prepare for the expected crash, getting a hole cut in the aircraft. It then dived into the sea and in crashing its bombs exploded. He was stunned but crawled out, got into the dinghy and put into it the other two survivors of the crew who could not swim. He then, by swimming, towed the dinghy away from the blazing aircraft and got into it. They were picked up in five hours. For fourteen days he was in a hospital ship which was frequently bombed. He could not sleep. He had a broken ankle and on reaching shore was treated for this and for nervous symptoms. When he left hospital he wanted to fly and tried, but on his first solo when his engine spluttered he panicked and made a forced landing. He was finally medically boarded permanently unfit for flying. He was given an office job in London where he worked during the period of heavy bombing. Throughout this time he suffered continuously from fear: he could not sleep; he was afraid to go out and arranged to live in the building where he worked; he felt as if paralysed when the siren sounded. In April, 1941, early one morning the building was hit. He was unhurt but went out into the street, walked over Westminster Bridge and saw London burning. His desire was to retaliate. With the help of friends secretly he began flying. Gradually he overcame his

fear, applied for a reboard and was officially allowed
to fly light aircraft. For a time he had to struggle with
fear, but after seeing a few crashes without fatal results
felt better. He was finally boarded fit for full duties
and returned to operational flying, feeling quite happy
and fit. Uppermost in his mind was the determination
to get his own back for the bombing of London.

I remember too, when my battalion was in trenches before Ypres, that a sergeant was sent away because his nerve
had gone. But at Poperinghe, with a train waiting to take
him to the base, he got out of the ambulance and tramped
back to the trenches.

I doubt, however, whether these men are more than
exceptions to the rule and I am fortified in my scepticism
by Symonds' experience in the Air Force in this war. He
has found that trying to patch up pilots who were not wearing well was on the whole unprofitable from the military
standpoint. It is better by careful selection and by raising
the pilot's resistance to fear to prevent his fall than to come
to his rescue after the event.

Nevertheless, for my part I do not question that pilots
ought to be rested after a certain number of hours in the
air. A policy of that kind may fail to bolster the wavering
airman so that he may fly again, but it is a source of hope
and therefore of strength to the average pilot, and must
stretch out his life as a flying man. This life is brief. A
General in the American Air Force said to me recently,
"After six months flying many pilots have aged ten years."
The alternative is to let a man go on flying until he breaks
and then to cut losses by getting rid of him—a policy that
is bad for the airman and demoralizing to his brother pilots.

The airman's need for rest explains the nature of courage.
It is the long drawn out exercise of control, which is three
parts of courage, that causes wear and tear. This is our
homely way of speaking of nervous fatigue, and this fatigue
can be measured. One day the barometer of courage will be

graduated and we shall be able to watch the glass rise and fall. The worker at his bench needs rest too for he is suffering from the same malady. How many hours in the day and how many days in the week can he work without staleness lowering production? And how much is the work of men of consequence in every walk of life slowed up by this blind industry? The crowds that are now clamouring for the seaside after four years of grinding toil are an expression of a want which can be met only by cancelling some hundreds of trains carrying essential supplies.

When, however, I affirm that cutting losses is a much neglected maxim of the soldier's creed I am not thinking of men who from prolonged service in the field or from exceptional stress in a single engagement are no longer battle-worthy. I have in mind only soldiers who never were battle-worthy. There is no sense in holding on to men without stability who are blown over by the first breath of battle. If a soldier is not cut out for war he should be scrapped forthwith for he spreads the contagion of defeat. It is not the number of soldiers, but their will to win which decides battles. In France in the last war when a battalion was ordered to send men to a Trench Mortar Company or a Machine Gun Corps it often seized the chance to get rid of its rubbish. These misfits of war were pushed from one unit to another, as in some card games we hurry to pass on the joker the moment we find it in our hand. Even in this war some of the drafts sent out to Libya were made up in this fashion.

I have said that the unstable soldier should be scrapped forthwith, but this must of course be done without creating an impression that a man has only to complain of his nerves to get out of the army. There in a sentence, half concealed, lies one of the major problems in the training of a national army. I was asked by the Canadian Minister of Defence to speak to some of his officers at Ottawa and when I had done he said, "What do you do with men who are in the army and never ought to be in it?" To this question there is, I suppose, no very satisfactory answer. Fighting units must be purged of these men, so much is certain, and since there are great objections to discharging them from the army the only course left open is to send them to labour battalions.

Sometimes it is not an individual soldier but a whole battalion that is at fault. In the only instance of the kind in my own experience I was not able for a long time to distinguish soldiers recovering from an exceptional ordeal in the field from others who should never have been taken into the army. My battalion, the 1st Royal Fusiliers, belonged to the 17th Brigade which in the autumn of 1915 was taken out of the sixth division and exchanged for a brigade of the 24th division. Our role was to stiffen a division of Kitchener's Army which had been badly mauled at Loos. It had been rushed up from the coast by forced marches and was thrown into the hell of battle without maps and in many cases without proper rations. Even when they got to Bethune a few miles from Loos hardly any of the officers knew where they were going or that in a few hours their battalions, which had never heard a shot fired in anger, would be in the thick of a modern action.

October 1915. In trenches at the Bluff—

I don't know what to make of these people. We left a division where nothing mattered but the good name of the Regiment and we found a mob. Barty Price has persuaded the Brigadier to leave the First in the line until the Kitchener battalion which is to relieve us has found its feet. He wants this battalion, officers and men, to come up in small detachments and get thoroughly familiar with the trenches. One or two of our people are disgruntled because this means a long spell in the trenches. They are disposed to criticize Barty Price and say that he overdoes the higher patriotism. "It is every unit for themselves out here. If he doesn't look after our interests who will? Besides," they say, "these damned people will never be any use to anyone." But the great majority say nothing. There is hardly any criticism of the 24th Division and the men just take things as they come. Nothing ever seems to worry them, though if you know them you can see they don't think much of amateur soldiers. But then they never expected anything from civvies. And what they saw at Hooge was just what they thought would happen if civvies took on this job.

I came back last night through the trenches of another battalion holding the line on our right. The sentries when they saw an officer approaching bobbed their heads up over the parapet and down again at once. "I spy" grinned my servant who was with me. It was a curious sight to eyes accustomed to see our fellows resting on the parapet at night as old sailors lean over the wall looking out to sea. And strange notices have begun to appear at odd places. "Dangerous" or "Under machine gun fire", and the guide will urge you not to tarry at some such spot because a sniper has it set. When we got back I overheard my servant unfolding the tale of the sentry to the other servants. "Gawd's truth," he added, "where 'ave these blokes come out of? They're scared pink."

Nearly a year passed before the 24th Division was thrown into the Somme, and in that time most of the battalions in the two Brigades which were hammered at Loos had recovered. But two battalions never got over that battle— probably their officers were to blame. Six months before the Somme that was common knowledge, but General Capper, whose energy had done much for the Division, could not bring himself to acknowledge that he had failed with these battalions. When in the Somme fighting they crumpled up leaving the units on their flank in the air, the Division paid in full the price of his failure to cut losses.

Chapter Eight

Exposure

What may have befallen the soul of the armies engaged in the winter campaigns of 1940 and 1941 in Russia is still hidden from us, though this may determine how long this war will last. When I try to guess I can only lean heavily on the past. It was the memoirs of Sergeant Burgoyne which first brought home to me how armies wilt when exposed to the elements. I learnt there how Napoleon's Grande Armée in the retreat from Moscow shook off its discipline like a coat of snow. The harsh violence of winter may find a flaw even in picked men. Captain Scott in his diary was concerned because some of his men were not wearing well in the long polar night. He writes "If we can get these people to run about at football all will be well. Anyway the return of the light should cure all ailments, physical and mental."

In the first winter of the last war the real enemy was the clay soil of Flanders.

> Winter under these conditions has a kind of petrifying effect on the mind. There is a peculiar blunting of impressions, a strange vacancy so that everything

78

after a time is accepted passively. Men are affected very differently. To the regular soldier it is part of the day's work, it is his business in life, a life spent soldiering in many lands, just a new station with greater precautions and more sentries. Even his officers are better fitted than most educated men to meet these conditions, for to an astonishing degree they are without curiosity or imagination, in fine, proof against the hundred and one things which plague a man out here and may end in his undoing. But in this battalion there are some who have not escaped so lightly. One fellow with a working imagination relapsed into a state of torpor not unlike the condition following intense grief, another drifted into a resentful state not easy to describe, which was the first warning of his defeat. Even officers of set purpose are not unscathed. In a service where individual markings are quickly lost, Barty Price after a quarter of a century in the Army had not yet acquired its complexion. To his brother officers the world they have known is the only conceivable world, everything in it is right and only some anarchists and a few funny people like that want it altered. Barty is one of the few. His head is full of questions which have never had any satisfactory answer in the life he has always led. He does not even look the part. His skin appears curiously dead and is lined like a trench map on parchment, in a fashion not often seen save in the very old, as if he had been dried up by the Indian sun. His hat has an exceptionally large peak and he wears it pressed down and tilted a little backward so that it seems to rest on his ears, which are large and stick out—exactly as Mike wears his, perhaps it is a vogue among horsemen. He always wears this hat, never removing it from the time he rises in the morning to the time he goes to bed, save for a little mannerism of raising it now and then and immediately replacing it, when his identity disc falls out, and you are a little surprised to find the hair is thick and quite black. His eyes are attractive, the eyes best seen beneath a wig, though he is in no sense judicial; they meet you with a steady, friendly gaze. But when the personal word passes in haste they will flicker and there is a strange shivering movement of the eyelids. The body is slight, the frame of a boy resting on legs as lean as Mike's but much longer, and at a glance you can see that he too is rarely off a horse. In the trenches when he has packed his subalterns off to their dug-outs to get some sleep it is his custom to share the night watches with his sergeant-major. About four o'clock he will turn in to sleep like a child and this has kept him sane through all these dreary months. He gives no sign of life till late next morning when he wakes suddenly just as he had fallen into sleep, and immediately lights a cigarette, gets up and calls for breakfast; when this is come he plays a little with it till the bacon floats in a yellow pool of egg, then pushes it from him and lights another cigarette. The cold he feels acutely though I have never seen him in a greatcoat. The men working cannot wear them and he will not be the comfortable foreman of a gang.

That first winter in the trenches was somehow different from anything that came after. Company commanders, fellows you could trust to pick up a serviceable hack at Tattersall's for a song, were encouraged to practise on their own as engineers. Trenches were drained as each man listed and without much help from the laws of nature. A battalion of sappers might indeed have fared no better, for material was scarce in those days. The communication trench which was nobody's child suffered most; early in December the water rose steadily and soon the trenches were cut off by day from battalion headquarters. So Barty was left all day to his own devices, he saw no one but the officers of his company—half a dozen boys taken from school or from Sandhurst and delivered to him in the raw state to be broken in. Unfortunately there was nothing in the military situation to fill the gap. Tactical problems there were none, only the winter. We held a straight line of trenches, we did not attack, we were not attacked.

Squatting over a brazier like some night watchman, he would spread out his hands in the smoke which curled up through his thin fingers that had a bluish tinge. All the winter when he was not in the trench he brooded, gazing into the smouldering charcoal as if he hoped to find there some solution to the riddle of life, where so much had always seemed to happen without any meaning. In peace time the barren existence of the soldier had hurt his mind and now at last when the chance had come to do something useful he was left there eating out his heart in a muddy ditch, doing a job which any sergeant could have done as well. And he was not built for this business. He hated to see anything hurt, it had taken him nearly a year, he once told me, to recover from the South African War. The *Westminster Gazette* was sent to him regularly but he never opened it. Two or three copies always lay on the table with the covers intact, like the pitiful collection of unopened letters that accumulate in the mess for a few days after a death. I thought of my father when his heart failed, and of my concern when I saw how he, who had spent his days reading, ceased to take an interest in anything, even neglecting the daily paper. Propped in a chair, he could not breathe lying down, he would sit day after day and night after night without complaining, staring in silence into the fire and often dropping asleep, to wake immediately with an anxious start.

It was not only the mind that was hurt, exposure left the soldier weaker in body and so weaker in purpose, his will has been sapped.

Armentières 1915.
The rain fell incessantly, day after day, week after

week. And if there was a break in the deluge the leaden pall just overhead that seemed to shut out all light and air left the impression that there had been nothing but rain since we came into those parts. Even in the farm where we had a roof over us that perpetual damp, that dreary flat expanse of monotonous country under the low and sombre sky began to oppress us. But up there in the trenches without cover, without any dug-outs to speak of, all day wading about in a foot of muddy water, wet to the skin, the men somehow managed to keep cheerful through it all.

We had been three weeks in trenches and there was no talk of going out. The Rifle Brigade who generally relieved us had gone into the line further north and there was no one else. The Brigade said they could not make troops.

One day there was a storm. It began I remember about stand-to, and by the afternoon the wind had risen to a gale. There seemed something spiteful about it, as a child works itself into a passion and in the end loses all control. I had been to the trenches and on my way back met the full force of the hurricane. It swept in violent squalls towards the German line, carrying before it sheets of icy rain that cut the face and left it tingling. I kept losing the track in the darkness and my feet often slid from under me in the mud. I stopped from time to time and turned my back to the gale to get breath. I was beginning to wonder if I had missed the farm when suddenly the great gate rose up in front of me not a yard away. Using all my strength I got my foot in and slipped through before it closed again with a great clang that shook everything.

Under the wall a knot of men were huddled together like animals in rain. They must have heard the gate slam and then the tap, tap of my stick as its iron top struck the bare walls while I groped a way along the narrow stone causeway that skirted the yard.

"'Ere 'e is. Make a way for the medical Horficer."

There was a shuffle and then an angry voice:

"That's it, stand on my bloody feet, yer bloody coo."

The man must have given a vicious shove for they went stumbling and swaying away.

Across a small passage an old and massive door gnawed by rats led down to a cellar; at the bottom of the steps a candle fluttered a moment and went out and immediately there floated up from that black nether-world a stream of foul oaths and wild threats.

The door banged behind me pushing me down into the darkness. I steadied myself and cautiously felt my way down the muddy and treacherous steps and at the bottom lit a match. The corporal pushed up a biscuit tin with his foot and fixed a candle to it with its own grease. The tin as he trundled it along made a hollow uncanny echoing sound. A sepulchral smell filled the gloom which at first hid everything, but when the eye became accustomed to the darkness there emerged a low roof supported by stone pillars down which the damp trickled, all so vague, so dim and ghostly it might have been a vault for the dead and that taper only a charm to ward off evil spirits. Straw had been thrown upon the stone floor and across one corner a stretcher guarded a well that sank through the floor.

" 'A' company sick. Abbott, Barnes, come along, get a move on", the Corporal shouted impatiently. "We haven't all night."

The candle flickered and blew every way with a curious wavering sound and when it seemed it must go out he pushed in a man and let the door bang behind him. They came down gingerly step by step limping painfully, hobbling away into the gloom beyond.

It seems now as if that pitiful procession was a dream, a trick of the tired mind. Long afterwards at Loos when they thought me asleep the story was told by my servant to some fellows who had been with us only a little while, and were now sick and waiting for darkness to go back to the ambulance. He told it perhaps to complete their education or simply to put it on record that the First Battalion had known better days.

"The boys just chucked themselves down on the straw and began to pop off to sleep in no time one after the other. But that there corporal 'e came and shook 'em. 'It ain't a bloody hotel, bed and breakfast, and don't you forget it' 'e shouted at 'em; 'im, wot lives in comfort. They sat up all stoopid like and started to pull off their boots and putties; a cruel business, it just gave 'em 'ell. And then they looked at their feet sort of curious. They couldn't make it out why they 'urt so. They wiped off the damp mud with their socks."

He had paused at that point and I thought he had finished his tale.

"You see most of the boys were a bit shamed of dirty feet."

His words brought back everything to me then, the damp air full of a pungent acrid human odour, the rattle of slates as the storm rose to a scream and always in the lulls the sad squelching sound of rain.

Perhaps the men were listening too, thinking of the trenches and of this clean dry straw. No doubt they imagined that most of them were for Armentières or even further back. And as I listened to the gale I found myself thinking of a night when I had sat in the darkness at the bottom of the trench with a man hit in the head, and had heard his breathing almost stop till it became inaudible and then rise gradually to a great heaving gasp. And this regular rise and fall went on till there was a pause when nothing followed and after a little I knew that he was dead.

"They are all ready, sir."

I started and pulled myself together and went and looked at their feet, red, swollen and deformed beneath their coat of mud. And as I bent to touch them they stretched back upon the straw hollowing their backs and making their limbs rigid that they might not cry out with the pain. It was all mechanical; no doctoring skill was needed there and presently my thoughts began to wander. I had a feeling among these fellows that in some way I stood for the existing order of things. I fancied that I was connected with and partly responsible for this pitiable sequel to all the rhetoric we were wont to hear before the war began. Little dry catch words and political tags, so incredibly futile now, passed through my head. One phrase that had done duty in the Radical press stuck like a blister: "The Triumph of Voluntarism".

Then the candle after a lot of jumping and flickering went out.

"Come in or get out, shut that blasted door."

It was the Corporal again. And when there was a light the shadowy forms of two men bearing a stretcher appeared on the stairs as if through a fog. They put it down at the bottom and taking off their caps wiped the sweat from their foreheads. From the edges of a big ground sheet that hid everything from view the rain dripped to the floor. The corporal took one edge gingerly and with a neat movement stripped the sheet from the stretcher so that the water fell harmlessly to the ground. There was a man underneath who had not long to live. His clothes were dripping and he lay in a pool of blood that might have been part rain. Lifting the stretcher they bore it to the far end of the cellar where the men lay on the floor.

"Gawd, if it ain't Bill."

The man on the stretcher looked at them, clearly he was at a loss to know what these fellows were doing there. And they too appeared a little taken aback and even sheepish, for they knew that nothing but a bullet or a bit of shell could have brought him there. When he had glanced at them his eyes closed again and in a few minutes he died. When the men saw that he was gone they sat up and there was a rustling of straw as they fumbled with their boots. And when they could not get into them one fellow with a big jaw got up and carrying his boots and puttees in his hand limped painfully away as a bather across the sharp shingle. Then the others watching him struggled to their feet, vanishing up the steps into the yard but the corporal followed them and rounded them up into a barn. There they herded together in little groups where the roof happened not to leak, listening in the darkness to the dismal howling of the storm.

"Are you all here?" I shouted, and they answered "Yes, sir."

"The Corporal will tell you who are for hospital, but most of you must carry on."

A gust of wind drowned my voice and I waited till it had passed. By the light of his torch I caught glimpses of faces that were drawn and expressionless.

"I know it's hell there," I added when I could be heard again, "but there's no one else and it's up to us to stick it."

A silence followed, then they began to move mechanically towards the door. There was a lull in the storm when raised and angry voices came from the yard.

"Leave 'em alone, Bert, they ain't no use, they're only civvies, they want their blooming nurses they do. They—"

Another squall caught the rest. The great gate slammed and I knew they had gone back. In the yard two undersized lads who had arrived with the last draft hung round the door attempting to explain to the corporal that it was no use, they could not get into their boots again.

"Can't you cut 'em like the rest?" he demanded roughly.

But I ordered him to take them to the cellar. That sort of stuff is not much use at this game.

In the farm Barty Price, who had come down from the trenches to see the Colonel, was drying himself before the kitchen fire. I told him what had happened.

"You see we're paid to do the job, Cockie."

But it had gone home. He picked up a paper and made a show of reading, but the muscles at the angle of his jaw were contracting rhythmically, and I noticed for the first time that he was middle-aged.

In the morning when I woke it was still raining, all that day it rained and when it was dark I went to the cellar to see the sick. But there were none.

In this war, the Army has not been asked to live in water-logged ditches. But the crews of many warships have been adrift in open boats or rafts on winter seas, without food and water, for days after their ship had been sunk. Surgeon-Captain Macdonald Critchley has told me that the behaviour of these crews in this ordeal depends on how they are led, on their moral fibre and on their race. If the master of the ship or a senior rating is in the boat, then provided he knows his job and can set a course, and looks after the comfort of his men, boldly assuming responsibility for everything, he will prove the salvation of that boat. He does things and spreads a feeling of purpose. There is a general desire to be like him, for in such a plight men revert to the instincts of the herd and crave leadership. When many survive it will be found they had such a leader.

The sailor's nationality too counts. Critchley writes:

The Anglo-Saxon comes creditably out of such an ordeal. From childhood he is brought up to look ask-ance at emotional display. Whatever happens, there is exacted from him a certain Roman rectitude of demeanour. On the other hand a Lascar crew, adrift in small boats, may quickly go to bits. They refuse to work, pilfer stores, and soon give way to despair, so that there is a heavy and early mortality.

We may ask if the Anglo-Saxon has always been a model in adversity. Old accounts of shipwreck read strangely to seafaring people nowadays, who take for granted that men under stress will act with decorum. We read of "shrieks of anguish and despair" and of "tears rolling down the faces of officers and men as they fling themselves on their knees in despairing prayer and supplication". Was there a different code of behaviour in those days or were the men of a different mental fibre, or are these accounts merely the conventional exaggeration of the writers of that time? We cannot say—we only know that these calls on the men of our race have become common, and we have seen how they have been answered.

Safely away from a sinking ship all sailors feel a sense of relief and even of elation. In races with few inhibitions this may be very plain and Surgeon-Lieutenant McDowall, D.S.C., has described the hilarious excitement of Italian sailors picked up after the Battle of Matapan.

But the English sailor in adversity is himself; he is given to a kind of facetious humour, witticisms pass from one boat to another, interspersed with singing which may go on for hours or even days. This boisterous mood passes as physical exhaustion increases. The men talk of the fate of their shipmates and officers; they speculate perhaps on the chances of being picked up. Hunger and thirst begin to fill their thoughts; like Arctic explorers they picture the meals they would order if they could. On these survivors adrift on the ocean an increasing loneliness descends; in their extremity they come closer to their mates, they share their feelings and their simple thoughts, so that if one man stands up his comrades may do the same. Then, as their discomforts mount, as hunger, thirst and pain increase, conversation becomes irksome, but they are not often depressed, perhaps as Hippocrates taught, there is a certain antagonism between physical and mental pain.

They grow quiet, they become taciturn, until at last they lapse into a state of apathy.

In the autumn of 1916 I wrote in my diary: "In a battle somehow the horror of this business of war is not felt. Nature has the stop on; perhaps we are half-doped to come through it at all." In this war Critchley has noticed in sailors the same mental viscosity—a kind of blinkers effect —while the danger lasts, so that only in retrospect does the full force of the ordeal emerge.

It is the grim determination not to die that brings the shipwrecked through their drawn-out ordeal: "We were convinced that good spirits were a better support than great bodily strength," Captain Inglefield wrote in 1782—only the will to survive can save sailors at the mercy of the North Atlantic after forty-eight hours without food or water. "Thoughts of my home kept me going." "Had I been single I'd not have survived." While we are told that "those that died, seemed to make no effort. They just lay at the bottom of the raft and gave up hope from the start."

On the afternoon of Saturday, 8th June, 1940, the aircraft carrier H.M.S. *Glorious* was within the Arctic Circle not far from the coast of Norway. At 3.50 the ship's company was ordered to action stations as contact had been made with the *Scharnhorst* and a cruiser of the Blucher class. At 4 o'clock the German vessels opened fire. Within an hour the *Glorious* received twelve direct hits. At 6 o'clock the signal "abandon ship" was given. The *Glorious* was then listing heavily to starboard and was down by the bows. The weather was bitterly cold and there was a long sea with breaking tops. The men swam to Carley floats which had been dropped over the side; it is not known how many succeeded in climbing on to these floats in the next two hours.

At first the overcrowded rafts were very low in the water, which in some of the floats reached to the men's waists. Some sat with one leg in the sea and the other in the bilge water. After some time their legs became numb, they were without power or sensation; it was as if "there was nothing below the waist", "they were treading upon balloons". Men did not feel hunger after the first day, but they were tormented by thirst, so that some drank their own water. The sky remained overcast, the cold grew more intense, the great seas abated. Those who fell asleep did not wake again. The will to keep awake seemed to run parallel with the will to keep alive, and sleep was the first sign that a man had abandoned the struggle with that fatal and overwhelming exhaustion. Men became quiet. They sagged into the bottom of the raft and sprawled with their eyes open and staring, their lips mumbling incoherently and their hands making feeble, useless movements. As men died they were tipped overboard to make more room on the raft; there came a time when physical weakness prevented the survivors from jettisoning the dead. A man said simply "I'm finished" and slipped overboard and was drowned. As men lost in the desert see mirages, the sailors suffered from hallucinations. One man saw in the distance warships in action, there were flashes and clouds of smoke; he pointed them out to his mates. Some said "Don't be daft", but others thought they also saw them. The ships were in view for hours but remained at the same distance. Another saw an aeroplane without any markings flying very low. He heard the engine though not at all distinctly. A petty officer had a vivid impression of a distant outline of a dockyard; there were many poplar trees, a long wall, and an aircraft carrier alongside a wharf. Ships seemed to be entering. This vision lasted fifteen minutes and then kept coming and going. He ordered the other men to pull towards it, but he could not say whether they also saw it. One sailor said he could see tankers and tramp steamers; his mate saw them too, but when they paddled towards them they vanished. He waved to two Swordfish aircraft that he said were overhead. Another sailor kept seeing visions of trees loaded with ripe juicy oranges. The sea had disappeared and he thought he was ashore. He tried to reach out and gather the fruit. He believed that others on the raft saw the fruit, judging by their gestures and behaviour.

The men copied one another. If one man stood up the others did the same, if one man waved his hand so did his mates. Suggestion had been given new powers by their distress.

It seemed that they had been on that raft for years. They were no more aware of thirst and cold, they did not think, they were in a maze, helpless, unable to do anything. They grew quiet and apathetic, their limbs had no life in them, their glazed eyes saw nothing, a low mumbling delirium was the only sign that they were still alive. One sailor who had been silent for nearly two days announced "I am just going to get a packet of fags", and stepping into the water was immediately drowned. There were four survivors of eighty sailors who had boarded one float; there were four left out of fifty on another, and on a third two out of thirty-seven were left alive.

Towards the end of the third day a sailor on one of the floats thought he saw a ship, he tried to wave a paddle, the ship drew nearer. A few of the ratings were able with help to clamber up the Jacob's ladders of the Norwegian trawler, the rest of the thirty-six survivors were carried aboard.

What is it in the spirit of the Navy that kept from quarrelling these tormented sailors whose reason had nearly gone after sixty-five hours adrift in the Arctic Circle?

Chapter Nine

At sea

A station commander in the Air Force knows how the pilots' will is burnt up in war. These pilots are the pick of our race, and it is his job to keep them in the air. He has not been brought up at the feet of his seniors, he lives in the present with its urgent demands, and if anyone can help him in his task he is ready to learn from him. That seems good sense.

But the Navy lives under the dominion of the past; it is far too robust to bother about a sailor's nerves. This confident mien is inevitable. The Senior Service has long occupied in the hearts of Englishmen the place reserved in Germany for their army. Where so much is slipshod and even humiliating, here, against a background of the rough sea, is a breed of men, doing a man's job about as well as it can be done. The Navy is efficient and it knows it is efficient. The traditions, loyalties and professional pride of the German soldier have here their counterpart. Besides, the Navy has other sources of strength. It is a picked service; of four ratings who present themselves at the recruiting offices the Navy accepts only one. Selection is at work too among officers. That a boy has set his heart on this tough service

goes for something. He has initiative; he is a cut above the
ordinary. Long before the Hitler Youth was thought of,
the Navy caught him young and soaked him in the pride
and joy of a great tradition. The ship herself helps; when
the time comes the sailor must fight it out whatever the
odds, there is no alternative, though I am told, some
Italians were so frightened at the Battle of Matapan that
they jumped overboard rather than fire a gun. But more
than anything else it is the influence of the machine which
keeps the Navy from going to seed in peace as soldiers are
apt to do. Every rating is a mechanic, there is purpose in
each day; he is intelligent rather than imaginative, he
thinks rather than feels about things.

Small wonder the Navy refuses to countenance nerves; in
conversation you do not hear that this man is not wearing
well or that another needs a rest, the subject is taboo. Yet
the sailor is not immortal; the nerve of three thousand
broke in the first war. And this war is grimmer and tougher
still; in a closed sea like the Mediterranean, bombing from
the air has given the sailor no peace. Moreover the rating
nowadays is often not a professional sailor. In three years
of war the Navy has grown threefold; of the officers who
broke down in 1940 only a sixth were sailors in time of
peace. There is another reason why so little is heard on a
battleship or cruiser of the ravages of war. It is the drawn
out strain of service on a small ship rather than the sharp
stress of a naval action which ends in defeat. Three-quarters
of those who were broken were serving in small ships. Life
in a destroyer in northern seas in winter must be rather
like trench warfare in a bad part of the line in the last war,
when the men were cold and wet and short of sleep; but
to the sailor's cup is added the physical discomfort of
rough seas, and the great stretches of time without shore
leave.

Youth—it is a young sailor's job—nine times out of ten
is undefeated by this battle with man and nature. But some-

times in the smaller craft ratings who have lost the resiliency of their early years are asked to meet the same calls on mind and body; if they have spent all their days at sea they generally come through the long ordeal, but if they have come back to the business of ships after years on shore they may be beaten. The crew of a minesweeper became unseaworthy in this war. Nine out of a crew of fifteen were more than forty years old. They had been kept too long on the same run—like keeping a battalion too long in the Ypres salient—and the enemy knew this run. They could neither look forward nor look back to any cheerful prospect. No one had ever shown interest in them or in their craft: they felt their isolation. They had no hope of leave, they wanted to sleep once without being called for a watch. And then, when the nerve of the captain and the senior rating had gone, there was no more fight left in the rest of the crew.

While then we give marks to the sailor because he does not babble as some soldiers do, it ought to be possible perhaps to speak of his infirmities without blasphemy.

Surgeon Commander McDowell, D.S.C., writes:

The strain of a sea fight leaves its immediate mark on the crew, they are keyed up, more emotional; they become talkative, irritable, boastful, quarrelsome and are given to harmless exaggeration, merry drinking, and easy laughter. Furious arguments, maddening remarks, petty annoyances sweep the Wardroom. At such times the example set by the officers as a class has an astonishing effect because one's emotional attachment to people is greatly increased. I saw the Captain of a ship drinking a cup of tea on the bridge in the course of dive-bombing attacks that had gone on all day. While he was drinking the look-out reported "Aircraft on the starboard bow, sir." He did not even look up. Then "Aircraft diving, sir," the Captain glanced up only. "Bomb released, sir," and the Captain gave the order "Hard a-starboard," and went on drinking his tea until the bomb hit the water nearby. The reaction to this episode was a kind of schoolboy hero-worship on the part of everyone who saw it. When the bombing had ceased the Captain went down to his cabin and when he was alone he wept.

This uprising of emotion may find vent in helpless anger; in cursing and swearing against the enemy during action and then in quieter times in violent threats against the foe, when ordinary men swear that they will never take a German prisoner. There is a great feeling of bellicosity among the ship's company; fighting ashore, quarrels on board, drunkenness, and irresponsible behaviour await the opportunity. Into a bar in Malta walked part of the crew of a destroyer that had recently arrived from Norway, pushing people aside and saying "Make way for the heroes of Narvik." In the bar were members of my ship's company who had been bombed frequently for six weeks. The battle royal which followed nicely illustrated the elation and aggression of the two crews.

How easily laughter comes under these conditions. A paltry sally will bring a burst of laughter which relieves the tenseness of the situation. At Benghazi there were very frequent raids, and an anti-aircraft cruiser that had been in for a few hours sailed out again to the shout of "Windy can't take it," from our crew. The too loud laugh that followed had not been forgotten by the cruiser six months later.

Emotional instability which is normal in times of strain makes the sailor very open to suggestion. The seed of loyalties, of national symbols, of tradition, of pride in the Navy is sown in this soil—the result is morale, the ability to do a job under any circumstances to the limit of one's capacity.

What I have written is based on my experience in two ships. One was sunk after surviving more than two hundred raids and the whole of the first Libyan campaign. The other was in four major actions in addition to many raids at sea and in harbour, and twice sustained actual damage. There were more than five hundred men in the two ships and of these only two came to me about their nerves.

Chapter Ten

The safe-keeping of the pilot

The pilot's life is forfeit if he mishandles his instruments, a single error may be fatal. He is too at war with nature; the hazards of flight still exact a heavy toll which he has to face without the bracing fellowship of danger that binds officers in a battalion to each other and to their men. The pilot is alone in the sky with his sharp foe. In a bomber his crew share his solitude, they cannot relieve it. He is not fortified by his duty to his men which in the infantry keeps an officer on his feet; he must always rely on his own skill, on his own resolution. He is without the support of numbers. In an impersonal war of millions he remains an individual.

A full-blooded statement of that kind can only stand with some qualification. Separate a pilot from his crew and both suffer. He may not be exceptional, but this air crew has become a little family; they have been together in tight places; they have come to depend on one another. And they are not always alone in the sky. Wing-Commander Gibson, who won the V.C. by bombing the Moehne and Eder dams from sixty feet, tells me that in that venture, in which eight out of sixteen aircraft were shot down, the pilots kept pushing away the stark loneliness of flying over sea and mountain by talking to each other on the radio.

The pilot may be shot down in flames; he may be pulled out only at the last moment. This fellow is thoroughly shaken, though it may be only for a short time. If he is not much hurt ten days leave will help him to his feet. If he is given longer he may begin to turn things over in his mind, and once that starts he is done, he will not return. There is a saying in the service "A man twice burnt is finished."

When I ask a station commander what strengthens the resolve of his pilots he answers always "leadership" and then after a pause often adds "and the quality of their equipment." These pilots reach out instinctively to anything that increases their chances of survival. Just as the soldier in the line puts his faith in generals who win battles, so the pilot requires of his squadron-leader that he does the job in hand without unnecessary loss of aircraft. The personal attributes of his leader hardly count, the test is in the air, nothing else matters. If he sets a bad example by not wanting to fly, if he is inefficient the spirits of the squadron fall. The pilot must see his leader in action, he will not accept his worth on the word of another station.

The rest is equipment. The pilot must feel that his craft is the best of its kind—many have not forgotten the devastating moral consequences in the last war of sending up mere boys in old buses that had no chance—he must feel that its armament is such that he fights at no disadvantage, for faulty weapons sap his confidence.

The bomber pilot has other enemies. In winter after his flight has set out in darkness for France and Germany a more formidable foe may creep between him and the base he left in clear weather. Twice in this war we have lost more bombers in a fog than the Germans have ever brought down in a single night. The first time bombers of the Northern Command left their stations at seven o'clock. The conditions were good, but about midnight a blanket of fog descended over England save for a few miles around the Firth of Forth. The pilots on their return were lost in space, many of them baled out in safety—yet the night had taken its toll of them, for a flight is more shaken by a catastrophe of this kind than by any number of casualties due to the enemy. It rots in the pilot's mind though he will not once speak of it. His faith in his ground organisation must be absolute, he should possess the assurance that a decision will be made in time to divert his craft to an aerodrome outside the belt of fog, that there will be no havering, no procrastination which may be fatal.

He should be as sure that his electrically heated clothing has no fault. At noon in high summer there may be thirty degrees of frost at a height of twenty thousand feet; at the same height in midwinter there may be sixty degrees of frost.

What can be done to make flight safe is done. Pilots often have to bale out over the Channel, and the efficiency of the steps taken to rescue them is part of their peace of mind. They sit on a small parcel which when blown up becomes a dinghy that will keep a man afloat for twenty-four hours. Small craft, speed boats, come to their rescue and on a day with good visibility when the sea is not choppy the pilot who is in the water for more than five minutes after baling out has a grievance. In one month alone—November, 1941 —a hundred pilots were saved by their dinghies.

But for every pilot drowned there must be a hundred who come to grief because their minds and bodies are slowed down when they become short of oxygen. As the pilot climbs the air gives him less oxygen than he needs; without his mask his power of decision and even of movement will eventually be lost. Every pilot ought to use his oxygen apparatus above ten thousand feet. Some flying officers affirm that they are not affected even as high as fifteen thousand feet, but their shooting at a target loses accuracy, and if asked to do simple arithmetic they often make mistakes. Many crashes for which no explanation was ever found were probably due to the pilots' air hunger. The mask must be efficient and it must be comfortable—if it is not comfortable the pilot pulls it off his face.

If he is careless about his mask he may suffer in mind and body from oxygen starvation without suspecting that anything is wrong, and his life may be cut short by the same misadventure. I want to rivet to the pilot's mind the picture left by Tissandier, the only survivor of a balloon ascent to 27,500 feet.

> The condition of topor which overcomes one is extraordinary: body and mind become feeble little by little, gradually and insensibly. There is no suffering, on the contrary one feels an inward joy. There is no thought of the dangerous position: one rises and is glad to be rising.

Since Tissandier's day there have been many workers in this field, but little has been added to Birley's account of the effect of this oxygen want on the pilots of the last war. The muscular weakness was such that pilots found difficulty in controlling their machines. The mind became inaccurate and lethargic; there was delay in making decisions or even complete inability to settle anything, rapid action was no longer possible. Judgment was impaired. The offensive spirit dwindled to nothing and there was a general disinclination to do anything more than wait about till it was time to fly home.

Here is his description of a flight landing after a high patrol:

> The gait of the pilots was unsteady and laboured. Reports were laboriously made out, there being general disagreement as to what was seen and done. Tempers were short. Everybody looked and felt tired. The idea uppermost in their minds was to lie down

and go to sleep. Their spirits were depressed; there was a deterioration in their mental and physical well being.

The resolution of a pilot rests on a multitude of small supports; each is kept in place by the sound instincts of his squadron leader. A flying officer should live in the mess, he should not live with his family. He will be with them when he should be with his brother pilots, he will lose his grip on his squadron as a leader of men. Nor does the softening influence of domestic ties help. The wife of a pilot who does not come back from a raid spreads her distress. We should not add to the pilot's burden.

Like the soldier he can be defeated by his own thoughts. Some measure of apprehension is indeed inevitable. Wing Commander Gibson writes: "Before a bombing raid while having a last cigarette in the office you are apprehensive. Then as you get into the plane and do things you forget this. But crossing the enemy coast brings it back though it soon passes. Then when you get to the target and see the cones of searchlights once more there is a feeling of apprehension. Again it vanishes as you do things. And when the target is left behind you relax. The worst thing is seeing the flak—the flashes. You must leave your imagination behind you or it will do you harm."

One night the pilot lives amongst civilians in soft security. The next he spends in a bomber over Germany. The sharp contrast adds to his troubles by keeping alive the idea of another way of life—the chronic danger of an alternative in war.

The fighter pilot waiting to go up is like a battery short circuiting; he is using up his will power. Casualties due to the enemy affect him less than crashes due to some unknown cause; he is disturbed when a good crew crashes into a hill without reason. Nine crews of picked pilots—experienced airmen who had, almost to a man, won decorations in the air in this war—were ordered to test a new type of aeroplane, but when four of the crews in succession crashed the remainder became ill at ease saying "Let's get back to the old engine." They would have endured such casualties at the hands of the Germans without a thought. Like a race horse the fighter pilot is a creature of moods.

The pilot's preoccupation with his equipment may be no more than a reasonable demand for the right tools, or it may be that the instinct of self-preservation is emerging and calling for help. Whatever the explanation this instinct, to which the airman offers so many affronts, colours his conduct in a dozen ways.

The moral fibre of the soldier, the sailor, and the airman is stretched by the same conditions—by loss of sleep and by fatigue. Night bombers often return from a raid about midnight, when the crews in turn are questioned at length, and an excited boy may take a long time to get to sleep. An experienced station-commander knows that eight hours of sleep are worth a glut of talk. He has not forgotten how pilots in France, immediately before Dunkirk, were fighting in the air most of the day and shifting equipment most of the night, so that the best of them soon began to show signs of wear. It is part of his faith that as long as a man sleeps he will not break; so he spaces the sorties of his pilots.

The mental strain of flying, Symonds has said, is precisely in proportion to the danger—fatigue is of less moment. The first and last cause of a pilot's collapse is a persistent state of fear. Therefore more pilots break in Bomber Command than in any other section of the Air Force. Again fighting in aircraft by day is less exacting than fighting by night, but it is more dangerous. So twice as many pilots come to grief as night fighters. In two-thirds of the pilots who had broken there was evidence of a flaw which was in-born: the way a man is made matters more than the risks he runs.

"Drink raises morale in a bomber squadron," a pilot said to me. He meant that after a raid where the losses have been particularly heavy "drinking with the boys" in some local pub over a game of darts keeps them from going off alone and getting into mischief, while it brings them closer together, welding them into one family. But drink, like any other form of licence, strips the pilot of the power to decide. Once that game starts it tells us that his control is going or has gone.

When I was reading for my Final I went one night to a music hall in the Edgware Road; after the small people had gone through their turns, Harry Lauder appeared. I cannot remember now what songs he sang, but when he had done I can see him step forward and then stand very still, his queer little figure all taut, while he gazed steadily and intently at the back of the theatre. So earnest was his look that it dominated his untidy features; you no longer saw the absurd little bonnet on his head, nor the great Irish blackthorn in his hand, nor the short bandy legs below the kilt; you looked only at his eyes. The laughter had stopped, it was so quiet that I heard a baby in the gallery whimper. He began to sing "Rocked in the cradle of the deep."

I thought of this incident when I was visiting a bomber station not long ago. The station commander had invited me to be present at the briefing of the air crews who were going to Brest that night. He jumped up on a wooden platform; his queer little figure was clothed in what is, I suppose, the Air Force version of battledress. His little nose, half flattened against his face—he was a Rugby international—separated eyes that looked so earnestly and intently over his nondescript audience. He was, I suppose, an insignificant little chap, but a stranger coming to the station would have known he was in command. I do not know if that air of authority is the outward sign of the qualities that put him in charge of men while still in the twenties, or the stamp imprinted on those into whose keeping is given the lives of others. It is common enough in the Air Force. The little fellow had no idea how to speak yet what he said seemed right. He told them it was extraordinarily important to the Navy that those German ships at Brest should not get into the Mediterranean. He knew they would do what they could to prevent that happening. It was extraordinarily important to keep to their times over the target. Then he told them about the weather they might expect and once more how extraordinarily important it was to get a hit on them. Then he jumped down.

I stood watching the crews trooping out into the keen wind that blew across the airfield. I asked about a big fellow with a ruddy face who had the look of a Naval officer. He was on the staff of Bomber Command, but he had asked if he could go in a bomber because he wanted to see for himself what they had to do. And now he seemed anxious not to get in the way of the crews in their preparations. He was one of thirty who did not come back. Some of the others hardly looked the part. Now and then when I visit a station the Commander, knowing what I am about, pushes me into a hut where there are twenty or thirty pilots and leaves me to get on with my business. When I glance round they are all looking at me as if to say who is this fellow and what is he up to, and when I speak to the nearest pilot the others all seem to be listening as he jerks out yes or no to my harmless talk, which sounds so stupid in this awkward silence. I wonder how long it will be before the Commander returns and I begin to tell them about Moscow to get them to talk. I have already picked out three pilots who do not look "tough guys"; I am always practising this game, but I am generally wrong. There is no type in the Air Force. It is no good trying to spot aces like yearlings merely by looking at them.

At half past six we walked across the airfield to a corner where the bombers were taking off one after another; it took twenty minutes to get them away, the ground staff of each plane waved as with a great roar it gathered speed. About half past ten I went to a room with a great window overlooking the ground where the aircraft would land. Messages began to come in from returning bombers; in one the brakes were broken and a quick decision had to be made whether it should be sent on to another aerodrome with a longer runway, another had a damaged under-carriage. The first was told to circle the aerodrome at 3,000 feet, the second at 1,000 feet until the way was clear for them to land. In another building the crews were being questioned, one pilot said that he saw a bomber come down in flames over the target, he described the incident as if he was speaking of a German machine. There was none of the talkativeness, exaggerated claims and too easy laughter so common in men who have just come out of action. You could not hear what they said unless you drew near to the table. The station commander hung about until four o'clock on the chance that more bombers would come in. As I was leaving the station next morning after breakfast I ran into him. "We took a pretty hard knock last night," he said, and then rather quickly, "But it must have been a grand show."

These pilots know the odds. What is it that makes them accept them without a murmur? Any high-spirited lad will take on a job full of hazard, but what keeps him to his task when he sees what it means? Many of them, of course, have the right temperament for the game. At Armentières in the first winter of the last war when the trenches were water-logged the men would clamber out of the trench, though the Boche was only two hundred yards across no man's land; it was maddening to lose some of our best people in this manner. They never gave a thought to danger, that was where they were different from the rest of us. They were casual; they were made that way and you could not change them. These pilots too are a casual lot. They don't bother too much about what may happen. They will not look at some switch which is vital to their safety before they start on a flight; they will not put on their oxygen mask in time.

This casual habit of mind helps them as it came to the assistance of my Cockney battalion before Ypres, but it is only part of the story. Once more I shall go to an infantry battalion for an explanation of the pilots' high resolve.

Ypres. September 1915—

The truth of war is written up all over these parts. Men know very little of what is happening outside their own battalion but one gets to know the people who hang on, and on the other hand tales come along of others less staunch. It is said that Pearson will not last, that Smith is angling for a job behind or that Meers is shortly going on leave and does not mean to come back if he can wangle it. A perceptible change of heart is abroad, there is a weakening of the resolve to stick by the regiment even among good fellows. Men hang on now, it has become a question of sticking it. I often think of the fellow in the Rouen restaurant who had suddenly blurted out, "The man who says he wants to go back into that hell is a liar." Is this after all the sum total of our modern equipment for meeting great adventures? Yet there are men who prefer the trenches to the base and the explanation is simple enough though I came to it late. At first it appeared that it was just because everyone likes the thing that he finds he does a bit better than the other fellow. He discovers that he is less frightened, that he gains kudos and in a sort of taken for granted fashion is held up as a pattern to others. Besides there is the intensely pleasant reaction after danger, the day after the battalion comes out of a big show, the first night in billets, leave. Certainly this love of kudos must be taken into account. It may be of the nature of frailty, or it may be only natural and human, but it is surely there no matter how artistically it is hidden. It is not however the whole tale. I doubt whether it greatly influences the elect whom I have in mind. What keeps them to the task in hand? Now and then an officer is sent to the base for a course, or to England with a wound, and it has happened sometimes on his return that he would say when we asked him if he had had a good time:

"Oh, yes, but I am glad to get back." Perhaps he would add: "They are such damned blighters at the base, you would wonder where all those poisonous people come from."

I know these fellows. They would not talk like that because it was the thing to say, but it seems incredible that anyone should want to come back to this life.

When you are in the trenches a cushy wound, a blighty business, seems the most desirable thing in the world, but when you are at the base the time comes sooner or later when you get restless and in the end you are glad to return. The good fellow knows there is something wrong with men who cling to jobs behind, he feels he is becoming one of them, loses his peace of mind and sees at last that in war there is but one thing to do, then he goes and does it, so that it is just a matter of time. Such a man however may and often does loathe every minute of this business.

Chapter Eleven

While one by one their moral props were knocked down

Χοῦτος τεθνηκὼς ἦν᾽ λόγῳ δέ σ᾽ ἐν βραχεῖ
τοῦτ᾽ ἐκδιδάξω πόλεμος οὐδέν᾽ ἄνδρ᾽ ἑκὼν
αἱρεῖ πονηρόν, ἀλλὰ τοὺς χρηστοὺς ἀεί.

Sophocles, *Philoctetes* 435-7.

As the war dragged on into the autumn of 1916, the German Army, like our own, had need of underpinning. But the lynch-pins were missing. A German soldier writes:

The tragedy of the Somme battle was that the best soldiers, the stoutest-hearted men were lost; their numbers were replaceable, their spiritual worth never could be.

Our own forces were in no better plight. Most of those who were meant by nature to lead men had been struck down by two years of war.

That is the story of all wars. A national army is held together by young leaders. They are most needed when weariness has dulled the first purpose of such a force in the third or fourth year of war. But as time passes they have

108

become scarce, for the best go first and have gone first since war began.

> Dead like the rest, for this is true;
> War never chooses an evil man but the good.

It is the theme of the *Iliad*. It runs through the humblest diary of the war.

> Just now a man was brought to my dug-out on a stretcher. Half his hand was gone, and his leg below the knee was crushed and broken. While his wounds were dressed he smoked, lighting a new cigarette from the stump of an old one. His eyes were as steady as a child's, only his lips were white. Afterwards he was carried away, the men looking on in silence. But when the ground-sheet flapped down again over the entrance, my servant grinned. "You always know the old 'uns," he said.

That weeding out of the best, as if the battalion was slowly but remorselessly being bled to death, was always going on. Some came to look on war as a sieve that let through only the dregs of men, as in Sparta the only mourners were the parents of the survivors. The one was taken, the other left; it is the substance of half my diary.

> There were two subalterns in another Brigade. Both lived for hunting and that sort of thing, while in their battalion the officers were mostly townsmen, city folk, people who travel in tubes, dull dogs to these two. It was not difficult to see that they were thoroughly tired of the war in general and of this battalion in particular. One of them, a boy with no means to speak of, heard when on leave that his elder brother, who was heir to the family place, had been killed in France; the way became open for everything he prized in life. When his leave expired he did not return; he went

E

sick. The other was Adjutant, he too went on leave about that time and worked an extension. Everyone said we had seen the last of him. His colonel was very angry and threatened hotly to stop all leave until these young cubs had learnt to play the game. But something in this boy's blood brought him back again, and that too before his extension was up. A week later he was killed.

The best of that generation have gone. They are dead. Excellent people there are still living, but there was a moment in their time in France, perhaps half forgotten, when the will to live was too strong, and that is why they are alive. We who are left know what fear is; they went out undefeated. "Their numbers were replaceable, their spiritual worth never could be."

A draft of seventeen officers came in October to fill the gap left in the companies by the Somme. The Boche had done his work with his usual thoroughness; we had to make a fresh start. "Anyway they won't be with us long," Hill had said when he inspected the draft. "I give the best of them two months."

Two months have gone and his verdict is in a fair way of proving true. The average subaltern, if he comes out now for the first time, does no more than sample war. A few, and these the more fortunate, were hit, happily before they showed signs of wear. And some went on leave and did not return, and some went sick, and some were discarded to trench mortars or in drafts to other Fusilier battalions.

But there were always a few good souls left over from a time before the manhood of England had been picked over.

It is strange how some good fellows keep on their feet, drifting back when their wounds are healed, like singed moths unable to leave a flame. Something in their stock tethers them to the life. They have seen this draft melt away and other drafts too, but when men speak of this they only smile saying that leave will come all the sooner. The value of these brave souls is beyond numbers, week by week they count for more. They are the backbone of every unit out here, the rest come and go but are never of us, only these remain, leavening the mass and making it possible to carry on. Without them I cannot think how an improvised army could endure so much.

Chapter Twelve

Thoughts that fester in the mind and bring defeat

"If these English had any apprehension they would run away." Does that saying still ring true in Libya as at Agincourt? And if not are we so changed that our imaginations run riot? Can it be said that we are defeated by our own thoughts? Are we not most fearful often when there is no danger?

This morning the Huns put a big shell into the little inn at the cross-roads and utterly demolished it, but it happened that we were out at the time. It made you think. You began to reason how easily you might have been there in the inn. You say "What luck, but can it last?" A dozen times you have escaped improbably until you are forced at last to realise the odds. The mind is full of what may come because it is full of what has gone. All danger is long past, but this does not mean that the imagination is out of hand, only that reason jogged by memory is presenting her bill.

There is another kind of fear in retrospect: where we were in great peril, but only felt it when the danger was past. It may be that anger stifled fear and then as the anger passed fear appeared.

Apprehension is fear in its infancy. There is no danger, so it has been labelled imaginative fear, but it has its roots in reason, it feeds on the memory of things. If a particular part of the line has begun to fret the mind it is because we have come to know the places that are shelled and wonder whether we shall get past unscathed. The Medical Officer of the 4th Battalion of the Black Watch, which was kept in the Ypres salient for fourteen months, has told us of the consequences:

> There was a feeling of tension, a feeling of jumpiness. Notwithstanding the work, the men had previously sung going up to the trenches and coming back, but they gave it up; they gave up all social business, they were getting into a state of nervous exhaustion. The troops were then moved to another part of the line and the moment they were moved you would not have known them for the same battalion.

"More life," Thomas Hardy writes, "may trickle out of men through thought than through a gaping wound." Even a road can make men jumpy: I find this note in my diary:

> It is foolish to be scared by a bit of road and dangerous to let the mind begin to play tricks. On the map it is marked as a second class road. Two carts might pass with care and the use of the grass by the roadside, but by day it is not used save by an odd runner. By night it is almost deserted; now and then approaching footsteps can be heard and someone passes by; he does not hurry for he will have to make a second journey that night and other nights too.
>
> I took a dislike to the road the night we took over. Where the ground fell away the bullets went by one's ears with a ping, and I caught myself ducking. Where

it rose to a ridge they seemed pleasantly low, swishing past so that men lingered at the spot, the fellow with me said, to get a Blighty one. And as he said this we tripped over a man lying face down in the middle of the road. He had picked up a spare and could not have been long dead, for he was still warm. It set one thinking. These random bullets have no particular target, but a little beyond at the cross roads, bare and exposed, you are in view of the Boche. Looking up at his line I often want to walk in the ditch which is broad and dry and well below road level. Then the road dips past the brick walls of Irish Farm, now about a man's height. The Colonel of the Leinsters had a dug-out near the farm and I often used to run into him mooning round. He had lost an arm by the shoulder and was not fit to come out again. The stump gave him no peace, but there is no holding some of these fellows, they must be in it. A week ago his dysentery flared up and he went out in a few days, his resistance had gone. Irish Farm is not a healthy place and I have a sense of relief whenever I get past. One morning I heard a big fellow coming and got into the ditch. It seemed to burst on the road near the Farm and not very far away. I waited for another but nothing happened, so I got out and pushed on. Past the bend there was a fresh crater half in the ditch, half in the road, the size of a 9.2 shell, and on the edge of the crater a man lay, half buried in the ground beside a dixie. I stayed beside him till they brought a stretcher. That night there was rain and the next day, and for many days after there was a muddy pool at the spot.

One night when it was getting dark and the ration parties were beginning to wander down the road Mackenzie was killed by a spare as he stood gossiping on the road by headquarters. In South Africa he had been shot through the head and had been invalided out of the Army. It had altered him, he took a long time to answer questions and had no memory to speak of. When it was said that Mac was coming out everyone was sorry for he was really not much use and it was felt that he would soon go out doing something unnecessary or even foolish, yet he was a brave soul and none better liked. War dealt shabbily with him, but in the end he went out undefeated. I happened to be near when he was killed and afterwards I hated this road more than ever.

Men drift into the dressing station at La Brique with a message or my mail or rations. They wander off again into the darkness perhaps to return a quarter of an hour later on a stretcher. Someone had stumbled over the body as it lay across the road, and now there is a rule that no one must go alone. Often during the night I am up four or five times. It always seems an odd ending to a soldier's life to go out carrying a few letters or a loaf of bread, and sometimes an officer stretching his legs will pick up a spare. One day you are just too late to run into a big crump meant for Irish Farm, and the next you wonder whether the whizz-bang on the cross-roads is a chance shot, or meant for you. When this has happened many times you begin to think. This road has played its part in breaking men, it has its own place in the scheme of things.

But in the last war such fears and forebodings were regarded as morbid and no proper subject for discussion in the mess. An officer was expected to suppress unhealthy sentiments of this kind as wanting in martial spirit and boring to his brother officers. He was to put them out of his mind and not to think of them again.. Usually he complied with convention and resolved henceforth to hide his fears. In that fashion he sat on the safety valve. Since he had no means of expressing those fears which threatened to be his undoing, they were driven down into the depths of his being and only came to the surface as battle dreams. Henry Head tells us of a pilot whose reason was shaken by terrifying dreams. He saw white birds at first in the extreme distance. They gradually came closer and closer to him.

He woke screaming and was afraid to go to sleep again. He had no idea what they meant, he feared he might be going out of his mind. This pilot had been shot down and the white birds represented the gradual approach of the white puffs of anti-aircraft shells. Step by step he was made to think out the meaning of his dream and the fear of the unknown went from him. From that time he was no longer afraid of the birds, though he had a natural fear of being shot down.

We cannot cleanse our thoughts of fear by repression of the doubts and hesitations which "occupy and mock the minds of men" in war. We have to put away any thought of an alternative to the dangerous situation in which we are. We must acknowledge that there is but one thing to do, then we shall go and do it.

But men are not concerned always with the safety of their own skins. It is not only their fate, but the jeopardy in which their friends are placed that jars their minds.

I have ceased to bother much about the odds, the chance of stopping something, but I have another infirmity now. I am for ever worrying about the people I really like. The Boche gunners have certain spots taped, but it is after dark that I begin to get uneasy. Every evening Barty Price starts off for the trenches walking up the Menin Road with an orderly and I cannot settle until I hear him return. I feel certain he will pick up a spare and come back on a stretcher done, and I often try to get him to go by day when it is—in spite of the attentions of their gunners—much safer.

But he only laughs. I lie reading by candle light and every time I hear a machine gun in the distance he comes into my head and I expect at any moment to see him carried in. The noise of footsteps in the street above brings my heart into my mouth and I say irritably "Why the devil does he play the fool like this?" When anyone gets a cushy wound I am overjoyed and make a mental calculation of the probable length of time he will be at the base or in England, right out of harm's way.

Chapter Thirteen

The battle of the Somme

22nd July, 1916.

The transport was already on trucks when the battalion arrived at Bailleul station and we got away without delay. The windows of four compartments in the last coach had been marked in white chalk for the company officers and there was another for headquarters. On the move again everyone was in high heart and we received frequent visits from Mike and Pat and Toby who came and went along the footboards. Hill and Mike and Toby are the only three people left of the officers who were with us in the first winter of the War. I had a corner seat and when I fell asleep there was still a great hubbub in the next compartment, and above it all Mike's laugh easily distinguishable through the partition.

23rd July.

This morning at a place called Longeau the R.T.O. roused us when he came for the warrant, and we began to tumble out shivering and half awake. Another train crawled into the opposite platform while we were forming up and a little later another. On some trucks a little distance away Boche prisoners were unloading wooden planks; the men looked curiously at them and one big fellow hitching up

his breeches spat upon the ground. The R.T.O. had told
Colonel Hancock that it was a fifteen mile march to Rien-
court. It was good to get away for a bit from trenches, from
all the dull monotony of trench life.

30th July.

The day began very early; the companies marched in
different directions up the hillside to practise taking
trenches that had been dug in the chalk by some division
which was here once and had gone and perhaps was no
longer a division. In the afternoon the little village where
none but the very old and very young were left was quite
deserted and seemed, as it rested in the hollow blinking
in the sun, to have slept for years. My work done I found a
track through the woods to a spot which looked down over
miles of golden cornfields, over the white road that would
take us one day to the business in hand. And there I lay on
my back and watched my horse browsing on the sweet grass.

By the inn I met Pat and Toby, they had put up some
jumps in a field and were off to slap their horses over or
through them. When we got back there was tea outside; a
bee was making a noisy tour of the garden that was ablaze
with flowers. We sat for a long time smoking in silence
until one by one the others got up and went indoors. The
hours slipped by, the light began to fail. The men in the
street scattered, but I could not bring myself to go indoors.
In the stillness and peace of the close of that long summer
day the little village seemed forgotten and had an air of
detachment such as we sometimes feel in the presence of
very old people who really belong to another time.

The church clock struck ten. I went out into the silent
street to the bridge by the mill and stood listening to the
noise of running water. An owl hooted in the trees by the
roadside that looked enormous in the light of the moon,
out of the gloom at their feet came now and then the clank-
ing of a halter ring or the rustling sounds of tethered horses.

Back to the cottage to sleep between sheets, the sleep that is kept for those who live in the open. We have been too long at this game to be restless. But orders have come, to-morrow we shall get to work.

31st July.

This morning the old people and their grandchildren came to their doors to wish us 'bonne chance' and with friendly eyes watched the battalion march out. The men joked and called to them in their own French and they smiled back a little wistfully but said nothing. The remains of a division went by. A sergeant marched at the head of one company which was about the size of a platoon. They were dusty and weary, but had the unmistakable bearing of troops who have come through a bad time and are out for a rest.

1st August.

This morning a short and thirsty tramp to the sand pits.

6th August.

We have been a week in the sand pits, nothing has happened. But to-night orders have come. To-morrow morning the colonel and the company commanders are to reconnoitre the line, the day after we shall take over from the second division.

7th August.

In these parts the quietest hours follow the dawn and it was still dark when we set out. The horses walked in single file along a track. The saddles, our clothes, the very air felt damp. We were silent, sleepy, or perhaps occupied with our own thoughts—it was quite peaceful and there was not very much stuff flying about. After leaving the horses at the edge of a wood we wandered for a long time through trenches. There was no life, animal or vegetable, in the utter desolation of that bleak charred plain with its black gibbets that once were woods. Nothing was left alive save a few weary battalions who were trying to snatch a little sleep hidden away in those deep trenches; the worn look on all the men's faces was the plain mark of a bad time.

9th August.

We took over trenches from Delville Wood to Waterlot Farm, which was only a name, the trench ran there through heaps of scattered brick; we had scarcely moved in when we lost a Company Commander. I went to tell Toby: Pat and he were inseparable. I found him making out a return for the brigade. When I had done he did not look up but sat without a word making holes in a piece of blotting paper with his pen. Then he said "Thanks, old thing," and went on writing. The night was quiet enough and we got some sleep.

10th August.

A bad day. In the middle of the morning some heavy stuff began to come over and I went down the trench to find out if it was doing any damage; almost at once I met Burdett who had taken over "B" Company when Pat was killed. "It's our God-damned guns. I can't make out what the hell they're up to," he exclaimed angrily. I pushed on down the trench and suddenly came upon the scene. The trench had gone and where it had been the ground was thrown up into mounds of freshly turned earth. Shells were bursting all round and in the black smoke men were digging. Muffled appeals for help, very faint and distant came out of the earth and maddened the men who dug harder than ever, and some throwing their spades away burrowed feverishly with their hands like terriers. It was difficult to get the earth away from one place where they said someone was buried without piling it where others were digging also. We were getting in each other's way. We were afraid too of injuring those buried heads with the shovels and always through our minds went the thought that it might be too late. Then there was a terrific noise, everything vanished for a moment, and when I could see again Dyson and the two men working beside him had disappeared. They were buried. And then as if they had achieved their purpose in blotting this boy suddenly the guns stopped. The men were angry; they had been let down; if this thing happened once it might happen again. Now that they could do no harm they thrust their spades viciously into the ground. I went along to the Colonel's dug-out. It was incredibly deep like a shaft, and on the last of the twenty steps he was sitting supporting his chin in his hands. "Hello, Doc., have you got 'em away?" he said. He spoke as of something that had happened a long time ago. He looked as if he had not slept for a week, and his eye blinked without stopping. It came to me then that he wasn't going to last.

"Doc., do you think you could give me anything for my dysentery." Perhaps he was too old for the job, or years of Indian heat had sweated the man out of him, or he was built for smaller occasions. In this business men grow overnight like plants under glass or shrivel as if nipped by the frost.

It was noon and all quiet save for the noise of our guns which never stopped. In the trench nothing could be seen but a great stretch of cloudless sky, only a glimpse, where the parapet had been knocked in, of the hollow to our left where Guillemont lay hidden in the shimmering heat.

11th August.

For two days we had been in those trenches, it seemed a week. When the Buffs relieved us we returned to Bernafy Wood. I had meant to go out with the last company but casualties drifted in, and it was nearly dark when I found myself in Longueval Alley with a score or more of trench mortar people. The Boche followed us down the trench as if their gunners were watching all our movements. Their shells fell so close they threw earth over the trench mortar men who came back in a rush towards me, and then as another shell burst behind them ran forward again like frightened cattle that push and jostle and are harried into the fields through the open gate by barking dogs. There was no officer with them, they were a mob. But fear which had so often lain hidden in my heart had gone from me. These animals given up to their brute instincts horrified me; that wild panic only left me with a surprising feeling of courage. Then there was a terrific noise, a smell of powder, and we were breathing black smoke; a shell had come into the trench, the fumes lifted and hung over the trench and drifted away and I was alone with my servant and a man lying in the trench without a hand.

These men were the refuse of a dozen units that had been ordered to detail men for service with this battery, and had sent these misfits of this time when men are men or nothing. Only Barty had given of his best. Lesser men had thought differently. This rabble was their doing.

13th-18th August.

Every night the battalion had gone up to dig trenches for the divisional attack on Guillemont. This perfect unit of the old army has been turned into a labour battalion; they have been shot down with their eyes on the ground and spades in their hands like prisoners who are made to dig their own grave.

15th August.

"My dysentery is damned bad, Doc.," the Colonel said, as he passed his hand through his thin hair as if brushing it back. And when I did not speak he went on: "I'm afraid I'll have to go sick. It's a nuisance, isn't it?" His long back bent forward, his head drooped. His eyes kept blinking. He looked old and troubled. For a quarter of a century he had been a soldier preparing no doubt for the real thing. It had come and this was the end.

18th August.

About noon we left Bernafy Wood to take up our new quarters in Trones Wood, a belt of splintered stumps. The

August sun burnt down out of a cloudless sky upon our little party so heavily laden with dressings and with rations and spare stretchers. The men soon tilted back their steel helmets as the sweat trickled down their brown faces and collected in beads on their noses. There was very little Boche shelling, only the constant stream of our stuff that passed overhead with a long, swishing sound. Three steps led to the shallow dug-out which had been an ammunition dump, and as we went down the stench of the place came up, catching the breath. Great shells were piled neatly against the walls on three sides just as the Huns had left it, but for some time it had been deserted and it was now full of tins and every kind of refuse.

At half past three, zero time, a tremendous noise broke out. Our artillery had never ceased pounding their trenches, now it seemed that every gun in France had opened on the Boche. The men grinned with glee and one big fellow, spitting on his hands, rubbed them on his hips. We sat listening to the din as if we would miss nothing of it. All at once the men ran out, in spite of the stuff that was falling all around; Boche prisoners were passing. The moral effect on our fellows was astonishing. I looked at my watch, it was exactly fifteen minutes after zero time. At the head of the prisoners was a German officer who halted and saluted whenever he met one of our officers moving up Longueval Alley. Then the string of Huns behind him, going along in their bandages with heads down, jolted into each other like trucks when the engine pulls up sharply and there was a lot of guttural murmuring. One or two wounded Buffs came in; they were full of these prisoners. They told how the Huns offered them money, wrist watches, cigarettes, all that they had; how they came out of their trenches with hands up immediately the barrage lifted; our men talked on and did not notice me dressing their wounds.

We had been listening tensely to catch through the din the rattle of machine guns, but there was none and very little rifle fire. The guns had done their job here and our conjectures were borne out by the appearance of the Boche prisoners. They had had a bad time. A runner arrived from the Buffs; "C" Company were wanted at once. The man knew very little, he thought the attack had been successful.

A few casualties straggled in, men hit in the immediate vicinity. The rest shunned the place which they could see was unhealthy. We questioned those who came to us while we dressed their wounds, but they knew nothing. Certainly there was less firing, the attack must be over and there was apparently no counter attack. But the perpetual din of our guns never ceased; after a time it made one irritable. What was happening up there? What had happened? Who was hit? This uncertainty was becoming intolerable. I went up the trench to higher ground where I could see a little of what was going on. The whole country seemed deserted. All the natural colours in that vast waste had blended into one neutral mask like the earthen face of a dying man, all but the deep blue of the summer sky that looked serenely down on this infinite destruction.

Hours passed, it was getting dark and still we knew nothing. I went down to headquarters for news, but they knew very little. We had succeeded in taking Guillemont station. The day they thought had gone well, but Milner, who had just got his commission and was still wearing a sergeant's coat, had been shot through the head at short range, and Rowe, who had gone back to duty from the stretcher bearers to try for a commission, had come down shot through the chest, and Babs was badly smashed up going over with "A" Company, and Barnes and Steele had been killed, and the best of the men seemed to have gone out. Somewhere up there out of reach, the battalion was slipping away and I could do nothing.

The faint light that filtered down the steps from the trench was failing and in the patch of sky above the steps a few stars came out. It grew cold and the human carpet of the dug-out quivered. Odd casualties drifted in, but the bearers and walking wounded generally gave the doomed place a wide berth. Hours went by and the Hun went on dropping shells around the dug-out. One big shell, it may have been a nine-inch, came over every quarter of an hour to the minute. We began to listen for it. We looked at the Boche ammunition, there must have been fifty big shells, this human dump when it went up would light the sky. There was a distant whirr, it grew louder and nearer and nearer and louder and then there was a fearful crump that shook the dug-out and put the candle out and threw a shower of earth that spattered down the three steps. And in the darkness we knew that we were safe from this gun at least for another quarter of an hour. It came so near it seemed as if the Boche gunner was playing with us. But this luck could not last, it was just a matter of time. We waited for a direct hit, but it seemed so inevitable that I had ceased to think about it. The shelling died down a little and the men dozed off. One of them, who was using his arm as a pillow, snored so loudly that he seemed always to be on the point of waking himself, but even when the heavy shell came over and shook everything he only moved restlessly in his sleep. Now that the light was coming I could see the roof dark with flies. I watched them for a while. When I turned over wearily my foot struck some food and a black cloud got up making a buzzing sound. There was a sour smell of sweat. Someone was shouting in his sleep, and then I must have slept too.

22nd August.

All around me are faces which sleep might not have visited for a week, they have dark shadows under eyes that are older, more serious. Some that were lined before look ill, and boys have lost their freshness in a month. Voices too are tired and the very gait of men has lost its spring. The sap has gone out of them, they are dried up. During break-

fast two officers of the 20th Division came into the dug-out
to take over. They looked so fresh and sleek and young they
might have stepped out of a hot bath after hunting. They
seemed to listen for shells though it was peaceful enough.
So it was true that we were to be relieved immediately, that
very afternoon we should go out to a camp in Happy Valley.
We were to march by platoons assembling at Carnoy where
the cookers with tea, the officers' horses, and buses for the
men would meet us. On the road we passed a Kitchener
Battalion going up, they were resting by the roadside.

"Them's the First," one of them remarked, and the men
catching the words straightened up and covered off.

It was a happy little family affair, that gathering in the
summer evening. The Somme was over, our little bit had
been well done and before us there was rest and perhaps
leave. It is these moments that make war possible. It is true
we have no traffic in heroes, but a good fellow means more
than he did. The mask we wear through life drops off leaving men as they really are. It almost seems indecent this
exposure of a man in the presence of his fellows, who for
the first time see him in all the nakedness of his natural
state. We are more critical than we were and a battle, by
carrying the weeding out process a little further, by raising
the standard of the tests, strengthens this bond between the
elect. You felt that night that people, the people who count,
were more kindly and friendly. Even the grooms who were
holding our horses looked up in an interested sort of way
and the transport men with cookers and buses greeted us as
people did on our first leave in February, 1915. Certainly it
was worth going through a show to come out of it. There was
a battle on up there, but we were at peace with all the world.

I stood watching the platoons coming slowly down the
valley to the hollow where the cookers were steaming. "A"
company had an officer and thirty-eight men, but their tails
were up, the effect of going over the top was apparent, they
were well pleased with themselves. "C" company had an

officer still in sergeant's kit and sixty men. They had sat for days under heavy shelling without leaving their trenches, the supreme cold-blooded test of this war. The difference was plain. Most of the old hands had gone out, here and there was an old face, but the best go first. The men stretched themselves on the grass with a mug of tea. Presently they clambered into the old buses, gay with the novelty of being carriage folk for a time, and we mounted and rode slowly away.

23rd August.

A blue sky and peace. But all day the camp in Happy Valley appeared to be deserted. When you looked into a tent everyone was asleep.

24th August.

From morning to evening the men sat about in the sun. No one did anything, no one wanted to do anything.

25th August.

We were not going very far afield after all. It was raining when we marched into the camp near the Albert-Amiens road, a camp in name only, for there was not a sign of a tent. On the far slope the men of the 73rd Brigade had been dismissed and were standing about like sheep in rain. A Staff Officer rolled up in a closed car. Hill, who had taken over command of the battalion explained.

"But the men have their waterproof sheets," the officer observed.

Hill looked at him, they could not understand one another.

26th August.

We waited on the road till a car passed which we stopped, and were taken into Amiens. These towns are strangely attractive with their French folk and their shops, after trench life and the eternal khaki. But this new zest in life is not so easily explained. It is more than contrast, Amiens is an adventure now. It is the old thrill of the Christmas visit to town and pantomime that seemed to have vanished for ever. We have become children again.

29th August.

There were rumours this morning that we had not done with the battle. It seems that a division is dipped twice into the Somme, with perhaps a week's rest and quiet sandwiched between. The second time it is kept in until it has no further fighting value.

31st August.

All day we have slept and lain about. It was peaceful here and we were sitting down to dinner in good heart when a runner went up to Toby and handed him a message.

"Damn them," he exclaimed, passing it on to Hill. Hill got up and standing with the crumpled bit of paper in his fist took a long drink at the soup.

"We must be ready to move off at eight sharp," he said; we had just ten minutes and the other officers hurried off to warn the companies. Hill told me we were to march by platoons to Pommières Redoubt, between Mametz and Montauban, to report to the 73rd Brigade Headquarters, where we should find out our destination.

The rain and traffic had played havoc with the road near Mametz and the wheels of the Maltese cart that was carrying spare stretchers stuck fast in the mud; we pushed and heaved and attempted with the stretcher poles to lever out the wheels, but nothing happened. We left it in the mud and pushed on to overtake the companies. At Brigade Headquarters we were told that the Battalion was taking over Carlton trench between High Wood and Delville Road; the companies they said had gone on some time ago.

We hurried on through the silence and desolation of Montauban. On that road which was usually so crowded with troops and transport we seemed that night to be the only living things. It was like being left out in no man's land, wounded, forgotten. Now that I had not the support of numbers I was full of apprehension. I had a feeling that something was about to happen. I wondered vaguely if it was the cold night air rising up out of the valley that made my teeth chatter.

A little beyond three horses lay across the road. The flies were busy with one of them whose intestines had gushed out; the horses were still bleeding, but the men with them had vanished. For some time we had noticed a strange smell and there was something that made our eyes prick; presently tears began to run down our cheeks. The road turned sharply to the left and dipped into a valley and all at once we appeared to be wading through a ground mist. Shells were coming over in great numbers. They detonated almost silently and without the burst of an ordinary shell. We had run into a gas shell barrage. I wanted to ask my servant if his chest felt as if it were being pressed in by an iron band that was gradually getting smaller. I wondered what gas they were using. I remembered we were told that many of the men had heart failure after the last attack.

A gunner came by spitting and rubbing his eyes. He said there was a sunken road a little further on which led to the quarry. He thought there was an aid post there; this was the land mark we had been told to look out for. We stumbled on and met an officer, hatless and supported under each armpit by two stretcher bearers. They said he was gassed and it may be that he was. Two winters he had been out here as a sergeant, a bold and efficient N.C.O. All last winter he felt the damp more and more and began to carry a flask. The damned stuff had done its work. "I wish to God I could get hit," he had once confided to me, "I am not the man I was." Now he was done.

There was a sound like coughing, it was coming nearer and then shadowy figures loomed up out of the fog. It was one of the companies. They did not know where they were, their guide had missed his way, they cursed him but he was lost. The gas was very thick here, it was unpleasant to the eyes and some of the men had difficulty with their breathing. We put on our gas helmets, but we could not make any progress in them in a country we had never been in before with guides who were so completely at sea. We should have liked to call a halt till the gas cleared, but we must have been urgently needed up there or they would not have sent for us like that, at a moment's notice; besides the whole place was being planted with these curiously silent shells that seemed so harmless. An officer near me impatiently tore off his mask "We shall never get there in these damned things," he said. I followed his example, I was no longer worrying about the gas. It was too late to do anything now. After all it was in our lungs, the thing was done, it did not really matter what the gas was; time would tell.

Apparently our batteries were everywhere, it was impossible in the darkness and in the fog to steer through them except by the flash of a gun as it fired. All the time I felt I was walking just in front of their muzzles and expected any minute to be blown into space. We appeared to be in a hollow, sometimes we seemed to be on the point of escaping on to higher ground, the gas became less dense and we grew quite hopeful. Then we were back again in the valley apparently making circles in the mist. We were in a maze and could not get out.

A man came up to me. He said he was choking and could not breathe. He clutched at his neck band and pulled frantically at it as if he would loosen something; he was terrified. When I had done with him we were alone again, the company had moved off to try a different direction. Once more we began to search despairingly for the sunken road. For hours we wandered aimlessly without plan or system. At length we both came to a stop as if by agreement. "It's no good, sir, we're stuck," my servant said, flapping his hands against his shoulder blades to get warm.

Just there the rising ground was fairly clear of gas, it was past three o'clock and we decided to wait for the light. The night lifted reluctantly as if it were loth to let us escape and the cold dawn had passed slowly into the promise of a summer day before we found Carlton trench. The last two companies had just arrived after eight hours pilgrimage in the gas to find that no one expected them or knew why they had come. The Colonels of five battalions were collected in one dug-out and the men were packed in the trench like herrings. It was clear we were not wanted, why then were we there? Hill answered tersely "Wind."

2nd September.

A day's rest has worked wonders. This morning everyone felt fitter. Orders have come from behind to rest everyone who was suffering from gas and the men knew that it was only necessary to report sick to be done with the Somme. A few—I could have given their names—came to me but the others insisted on carrying on, they would not leave the battalion while it was waiting to go over the top.

"What's the position really, Doc.?" Hill asked when we were alone. I hesitated a moment. If the men were all right we were apparently to do another attack. To say they were fit was like signing the death warrant of two hundred men. And I might be wrong.

"I think everyone is in the same boat, and if anyone carries on we all ought to."

"That's just what I think, Doc. The whole battalion can't go sick."

"I don't believe anything will happen if we do carry on," I said at last.

"Well," said Hill, "that settles it, I'll tell the Brigade," and he went off.

4th September.

The Corps gas expert has apparently paid us a flying visit to report on the effects of the gas on the men. I did not hear of his visit till he had gone and the men with whom he talked, now that they had got hold of one of those people from behind, rather enjoyed making his hair stand on end. What they told him has not transpired, but it seems that since his report the Corps is unwilling to use the battalion again in this battle.

5th September.

Before breakfast Hill handed me a message from the Brigade.

"You see, Doc., old Roger Rum has settled it for us. He's had enough."

"He's going to use this gas business as an excuse?"

"It looks like it."

"The sly old fox."

"Besides," Hill added, "he isn't the only Brigadier who has had his fill. I hear old Caxton says he won't be responsible for what may happen as his men are exhausted."

A runner came up, saluted and handed Hill a message. He smiled as he read it.

"We weren't far wrong. The Division is to go out immediately and the 56th will take over from us this afternoon. We go back to Happy Valley."

The Somme as far as we were concerned was over.

6th September.

The country seen from the train changed as we left the battle zone, every moment it became greener and less dusty. It was like the journey home from school for the summer holidays.

It was late when we arrived at Longpré. There seemed somehow a strange peace in the silence of the night as we marched through the deserted streets of the sleeping village; across the Somme like a silver streak seen by the full moon; between great trees which lined the road and formed black silhouettes against the sky. It was good to see these fellows so happy and lighthearted as they swung along singing, and later there was the silent trudge and tramp of weary men.

Chapter Fourteen

A trench raid

Here and there the earth showed through the snow that covered the plain; against the black horizon, where there was more snow coming, the remains of Loos stood up stark and desolate. No living thing caught the eye, no sound broke the silence, nothing moved, and in this ominous stillness one had a feeling that something was about to happen. The piercing cold made the bones ache and now and then a flake of snow drifted hesitatingly through the air.

I shivered and turned back and saw the Colonel walking over the snow towards me. His hands were buried in the deep pockets of his riding breeches and his shoulders were raised as if he felt the cold.

"Good morning, Doc." And when he had said this he seemed awkward as if he had something to say to me and did not know how to say it.

At last he blurted out "Doc, we've got to do a raid, the Corps want us to send over a hundred and twenty men with eight stretcher bearers."

"At night?"

"Yes, they are going to have a preliminary bombardment and gas."

"Good God, to warn the Boche we're coming?"

The Colonel laughed awkwardly. "It's damned silly I know, but we've got to do it Doc. And what can I do?" He looked so old, so cold and miserable that for a moment I forgot his incompetence and was sorry for him.

"If you will leave the wounded to me, sir, I'll see to them." He seemed to breathe more freely. He did not question how I proposed to do it, he was only too glad to shelve some of the responsibility. He hated responsibility.

"Thank 'ee, Doc. Then we can leave it all to you?"

He stood for a moment as if he ought to say something more, but when I said nothing he went away.

The raiding party had been taken out of the trenches and sent back to Mazingarbe for rehearsals. Since I had promised the Colonel to go with them I could not settle to anything; as the battalion was in the support line and there was nothing for me to do I decided to pay a visit to the raiders to talk things over with the four officers who were going with them. I found them sitting in their billet doing nothing.

"Do you think anything can come of this business, Doc.?"

"I don't see why not."

"Honestly, Doc. Do you think these raids do any good?"

"God knows, they say they do."

"Who's they, the brass hats you mean?"

"Yes."

"No one in the trenches thinks they do."

"You must remember we only see one side of them. We see . . ." I stopped short.

"The casualties? Eh?"

"Sometimes there are hardly any."

The spotted subaltern who had sat silent got up.

"Well, it's no good getting the wind up, and that's all there is to it. I'm all for getting it over."

Once when I was a boy another lad, who was carrying a mouse by its tail, said to me, "Come and see me feed my owl," and threw the mouse between the bars into the cage. It sat there as if petrified, it made no attempt to escape and the owl only blinked at it and did nothing. Suddenly the mouse moved and the owl with a quick movement bit off half its tail. The mouse squealed and then sat quite still again with its red stump of a tail and I came away in disgust. And these four boys sat there in their little cage of a billet making pictures in their poor frightened minds while the Boche up there blinked and waited patiently for them to make the move.

The morning of the raid when the Colonel's servant went to call him he found him walking about the dug-out. He had not slept well and was glad to be up.

"Where's the wind?" he asked at once, and then, impatiently:

"Go and find out at once."

The day passes slowly. A dozen times in the past hour I have got up and gone out into the trench. The men who form the raiding party are coming along Northern Up from Mazingarbe; they sing and joke and are full of themselves.

It is freezing. Now that I am certain what I ought to do I am conscious of a feeling of exhilaration that is not common in trench warfare. An hour's tramp along the footboards, we twist and wind round traverses, through interminable communication trenches which seem curiously deserted. Not a shot can be heard in the silence of the frosty night, and we do not altogether like this strange peacefulness.

It is ten-fifteen, nineteen minutes more. We are still held up by the line of raiders waiting for their bombs. It seems impossible for them to be in time. Then we climb out of the trench and get past and in a few minutes are in the front line. This is the point where the raiders leave the trench, and already I can see figures beyond the parapet silhouetted against the sky; they stoop, dart a few yards forward and stoop again, their job is to cut our wire to let the raiders through.

Everything seems ready, but my servant runs after me, we have forgotten the white armlets the raiders wear to prevent mistakes in the Hun trench in the darkness amidst the inevitable confusion; a bandage quickly puts that right. The raiders are filing into the trench and we go down a few steps into the dug-out to get out of the way.

The Boche is uncannily quiet; in the old days we should have said he was up to mischief. Is he expecting us over there? It is ten-thirty by my watch, in four minutes our artillery will open, the heavies on their batteries, the field guns on his front line. There is a sudden swishing sound of whizzbang stuff overhead, followed by the lower ripple of the heavies; from the steps of the deep dug-out it sounds quite a respectable bombardment, and presently there are flashes across the mouth of the dug-out as Hun shells burst over our heads.

Now it is ten-forty, the last man must be out of the trench and then as we stand and watch these Boche shells bursting and listen to their rending explosions, suddenly and without warning I am seized with an overpowering desire to await the raiders return here in this deep dug-out with its immense sense of security.

"Damn."

"Anything wrong, sir?"

"No, but it's time we got a move on."

Then we climb out of the trench and get through the gap in our wire and I forget all about the moment on the stairs.

There are plenty of friendly shell-holes and we get into one about half-way across and lie flat. Yesterday's snow still whitens the level ground; all the way across at intervals of about fifteen yards little parties of three lie in shell holes peering ahead with their rifles ready. The Hun shelling has stopped and there is a curious absence of bullets. But

the swishing sound overhead never ceases; one of our guns
is firing persistently short in the middle of no man's land;
the shells burst in the same place every time. There is a
flash of light, a little black cloud in the air and the men
instinctively crouch down into their shell holes. Twice it
has burst over us but no one is hit; evidently it was deton-
ating too high in the air to do much damage.

"That's a bomb, sir, they're in."

We crawl forward and come upon a sap, its position has
been carefully explained to us with photographs taken from
the air; we must be quite near the Hun line. The heavies
had taken on this sap three days ago, they had done the job
pretty thoroughly. In this light it has the appearance of a
sappers' dump with its broken planks, its bits of wood, and
litter. Following the sap we come to the Boche wire and find
at once the gap that the guns have cut, here the wire is no
longer much of an obstacle, but the broken strands tear
one's puttees.

Suddenly a man springs to his feet out of a shell hole
and challenges us all in one action, he is very excited and
holds his bayonet uncomfortably near my person. The corporal with me tells him not to be a fool and gives me a grin.
Certainly some of these fellows lying out here in no man's
land have the wind up and my senses too seem on the
stretch, a hundred thoughts run through my head. I keep
noticing little trifling things as if all these months in France
I had been half asleep and the raid had shaken me awake. It
is surprising how much can be seen out here in the snow. In
the trench it seemed dark enough.

And this is the Boche trench. Now that we are actually
in it we are a little surprised to find it so like our own. At
this point where the raiders have entered the German
trench a little party has been stationed. They are very much
on the alert and it is as well to warn them that we are friends
before we jump down. There is quite a lot of bombing going on to our right and to our left and already men are

returning down the trench, some limping and some with an arm round the necks of two pals. We do not let them stop to dress their wounds but send them on at once across no man's land.

No one knows what is happening; these four diverging trenches, that lead from this point towards the Boche support line, bend almost at once round traverses beyond which nothing can be seen. We expect every moment to see a Hun bombing party appear round a traverse; we think, too, it would not be easy in the gloom of the trench to distinguish friend from foe till they are right on top of us.

And now it is beginning to dawn upon me that I am only a spectator of all this infinite confusion. Twenty men might be lying there wounded in the darkness at the bottom of the Boche trench and none could know until the raiders are checked when we return. And then it will be too late. The Brigade had been a little doubtful about my plans, and to get my way I had said curtly "Do you think I would take this on if I didn't know I could do it?" If the men who are not hit keep their heads it will be all right. If not . . . well, it's too late now.

Figures seem to be constantly leaving the trench and returning across no man's land, in the direction of our line. I begin to feel isolated in this Hun trench; after all, only a mere handful of the raiders can be left on this side now, while somewhere not many yards away there is a whole Boche battalion. Three prisoners come round a traverse with their hands up, two are wounded. They are badly rattled and one of them is absurdly young. Obviously they are concerned about their safety, they climb out of the trench without any encouragement and hurry through the gap in their wire, heads down. We watch them till it is no longer possible to see anything. Quite a number of our men appear to consider it necessary to accompany them across no man's land and I wonder again how many of us are left now on this side. More wounded dribble down the trench and are helped through the wire, then a yellow light goes up, the signal to retire. My heart stands still, for a moment I think that something has gone wrong or that the Boche is coming. Surely we cannot have been in the Hun trenches for forty minutes.

Now everyone is hurrying back across no-man's-land, their pace varying with their morale. It is surprising how few seem to be left on this side. A bunch of raiders has collected round the gap in our wire as if it were a turnstile. The last man is in now and we get down into the trench asking anxiously if anyone is missing. But it is impossible to get any information; some of the raiders are streaming into Railway Alley talking rapidly to each other, others are limping away towards the dressing station, while beyond, two sentries of the 12th Fusiliers, who are holding these trenches, appear strangely still and detached amidst the excitement and animation of our men. Even in this light I know at once when they mix with our men, which of them has been over the top. The Boche guns open on the communication trench, there is less talking and the men scatter quickly.

One of the Boche prisoners is seated on the ground by the entrance to the dug-out; he is a poor specimen, undersized and frightened, and now with his head resting on his chest and his arms lying loosely across his thighs, sitting there all crumpled up, he might be a spent runner. He looks up quickly as a stretcher bearer approaches him, his boy's face covered with blood and blackened by the explosion of a bomb. And when he sees the open clasp knife he shrieks "Hans, Hans", and falls upon his knees. Then the bearer with a grin begins to slit up his clothing to get at his wounds. Someone says there is a man on the steps who looks "rotten", I go at once but he is dead. From the trench above a voice calls down to clear the way for a wounded man. The dead man is pulled anyhow down the steps into the dug-out and a big fellow is carried in. He has not long to live, but his blood is still hot and he rallies at the sight of a Boche. He contrives with a last effort to turn his head, spitting out a stream of curses at the little Hun who is very frightened and does not see that the Englishman's fighting day is over.

A man's voice is busy explaining how he himself had killed six Boche. Above all the noise comes a cry for water. On the ground at my feet a man is spread on his face with outstretched arms, his shirt has been ripped up to get to his wound, laying bare the great rippling muscles of his shoulders and of his immense back. Beside him another big fellow all huddled up is propped against the wall of the dug-out, his head has dropped on his shoulders and like a great doll that will not sit upright he keeps slipping down and is as often put back.

There is blood everywhere, all other smells are drowned by its stench. Fumes from a coke brazier fill the place and make men cough when they come in out of the fresh night air. Nothing is left in the dug-out but bits of clothing and equipment and dirty bloody dressings with odd rifles and boots and a few tin hats and gas helmets. The last wounded man has gone now and we are glad to escape into the clean frosty air. The trench is deserted except for those two sentries who have not shared in the excitement and the kudos, who have still four more days in these trenches before they go out to rest. All is as quiet now as it was an hour ago before we roused the Boche, the little burst of activity has died down as suddenly as it began.

In the Colonel's dug-out it is difficult to move, everyone wishes to report to him at once, but he is busy with his account of the raid which the Brigade must have immediately. They want something that they can improve upon and serve up to the Division, who in turn will pass it on to the Corps adding a little extra colouring. The little that I know is quickly told: thirty-one men were brought back across no man's land: not a single wounded man was left behind. These fellows have played the game. I shall not wait for the Colonel who will be a long time over this report. He is an indifferent journalist and has not been instructed in his youth in the art of making much out of little.

Very early this morning while we were still asleep General Capper entered the dug-out. He was full of the raid which he said had been a great success. He warmly congratulated the Colonel who ventured to say that it had been very expensive. The General told him that he must not worry about that and asserted that we had killed and wounded many more Boche. He had just come from the raiding party where he was told that the men had asked if he was coming to visit them. Evidently this had pleased him for he was in great good humour. When he had gone we turned over and were asleep almost before he had left the dug-out.

Chapter Fifteen

Monotony

It was not, I think, until the summer of 1916 that I began to be disturbed by the effect of monotony on men's minds. Before the Somme I had accepted it as natural, and even inevitable, when intelligent human beings were thrown into ditches that were mere stagnant drains in which the youth of England was rotting. Monotony was a form of suffering reserved for active minds, which crave food like hungry bodies. But the winter of 1917, as I have said, broke on an Army in France, still shaken by the battle of the Somme, and it became plain that we must come to grips with this plague if men were to keep afloat.

I had been so intent on the forces which contributed to individual defeat that I had failed to understand how men did, in fact, contrive to last out in the trenches. Apathy, an almost universal torpor, was a wall of defence set up by nature to meet the violence of the hour. It kept at arm's length the habit of introspection, which was the sure and certain herald of individual defeat. It was an insurance which men took out against the unhinging of their minds. Sometimes it had strange consequences. Though time hung on our hands, only a few found refuge in books. By every post came parcels, but eatables, always eatables. There were no books in the mess. Men who had been voracious readers said they could not settle to read; there was a habit easily acquired by just doing nothing. For more than two years I was with a battalion in France, with little to do, and in that time I read only one book—Conrad's *Mirror of the Sea* met my mood, and I knew it almost by heart before the end of 1916. Later, with the Cavalry, I began to read like a man after a long illness.

When we did think, we lived in the past, for it was clearly unwise to live in the present. We could only cheat our present distress by a flight into other times, away from all the dreary tribulations of the passing hour.

Only humour helped. Humour that made a mock of life and scoffed at our own frailty. Humour that touched everything with ridicule and had taken the bite out of the last thing, death. It was a working philosophy that carried us through the day, a kind of detachment from the "insubstantial pageant of the world". But this gift of humour which encased our cockneys like chain-armour was not to be found among the Australians and Canadians. Perhaps nations in their infancy cannot afford to laugh at themselves. Perhaps it is the expression of an older race, a little weary, that is no longer eager for adventure and has lost the zest which had once taken it out into new places.

More was needed. I turned back to the manner in which men had daubed patches of colour upon the pale surface of their lives before the war uprooted them. There are some who contrive to dodge the burden of life by their own ingenuity. They never grow up, they remain big children. Where the rest of us conform at last to the life around us, and bow to its decrees, they live in a more friendly world of their own making. Their difficulties are solved and their desires met, not by a crude effort of the will, but by the easy turn of their fancy; these men are dreamers. But war deals summarily with the individual; it presses hardly on the man who leaves the herd.

These happy few exist apart; for most men there is no rest, no peace of mind, without an end in view; something to achieve, something always in time to come which can make the present endurable. They had once borrowed hope from the future, but in war there was no future. At Armentières in the first winter I cannot remember thinking that life was monotonous. It was novel, eventful; though nothing ever happened, I kept thinking that something was about to happen. But the winter of 1917, the third out here, seemed interminable; the awful sameness of the days fastened on to the mind, till I prayed that something, that anything might happen; but nothing did happen, until at last I had given up anticipating anything.

There was in boredom a desire for change, a state of rebellion, discontent. In that first winter it seemed that there was only one thing to do and I was doing it, my mind was full of peace and a contentment that I had not known before the war. Discontent could only be met by the preservation in its integrity of the idea greater than fear that kept men to the task in hand—by 1917 that anchor had begun to drag. We were less certain of things, alternatives had crept into the mind, there was still only one thing to do, but not everyone was doing it. I had come at last to brush aside easy explanations offered by the life around us. Monotony was fatigue, a sickness of the mind. I had asked myself at what stage in a man's life in the trenches he begins to be plagued in this fashion, and it came to me quite suddenly that the complaining man was the man who was not wearing well, that boredom was a symptom and not a cause of unrest. It was the man himself and not the life he led that was at fault.

Chapter Sixteen

Death

Dying men rarely experience pain or apprehension, or terror or remorse; their lives peter to an end, "like their birth, their death is a sleep and a forgetting". When death is not far off, when a wounded soldier lies very still on his stretcher, when old age or mortal illness have laid their hands on men, nature with a kindly gesture dulls the senses, and death like a narcotic comes to steal men almost in their sleep.

Old people with slow thoughts pass beyond the doubts and fears and hesitations of their middle years into the silence of great age, and when at last death comes to them quietly they hardly know their friendly visitor. Arteries harden, blanching the seat of reason; men see life dimly as through a film, and find on the brink of dissolution the peace that passeth all understanding.

I can remember a man who had taken poison, and I was brought to him too late to help. In the tumult of that house he remained calm. He did not appear to feel bodily pain or to suffer anguish of the mind. He was not concerned. He belonged to this world only by courtesy.

I remember too that in my years in France I had seen

only one of many soldiers wounded unto death who was afraid to die. The men of his company would do anything for him, which is another way of saying that he was no coward. Hit early one morning he was taken to a broken-down farm not far distant, and I was with him until he died many hours later. Though gravely hurt and in great pain he kept cheerful and patient without complaint. He was so certain he was going to get well—he said as much—but a few hours later, when he was worse, it suddenly occurred to him that he was done. He took my hand in terror and whispered, "Am I going to die?" I got up and put a heavy box of dressings against the door.

We who practise physic are compelled to witness things which no man should be asked to face. The wounds we dress are nothing, it is when something has gone in the make-up of a man that this bloody business comes home.

Yet the last thoughts of dying men are not my text. Death has no part in these pages save as a menace to the soldier's peace of mind when he is still in the rude health of his years. It is not death but the soldier's attitude to death which is my theme.

In time of peace men meet death but once or twice in a lifetime, yet doctors could hardly live if it were not for the fear of death; it gets into a man's mind when his youth has gone like the death-watch beetle in old timber. In war men meet death daily and in every shape. Nevertheless it is kept from their thoughts by an intuition that so only can they win their secret battle with fear. When men's minds were obsessed with death they did not wait to meet it. This was the way of safety and youth met the threat with their own weapons, humour and mockery and such cold comfort as they could find in leaving this world before their powers began to wane. Besides war is the business of youth and no young man thinks he can ever die.

This came into my mind one day in the autumn of 1916 when, during leave, I read Lord Morley's *Recollections*, "I find my dislike to the thought of extinction increasing as I get older and nearer the grave." So Huxley, and Spencer, the agnostic, in reference to his funeral—"I do not like the thought of entire silence." Is not the fear of dying often keener than the fear of death? But that men who have pondered on ultimate things should await death in that mind seemed strange. I found when I read of death that I had thought very little about it. Once, it is true, I remember destroying a little rubber doll taken from a cracker because I thought it would appear ridiculous if my pockets were turned out, as might happen any day. And twice I made a will: once before the Somme, when I gave the post corporal who lived with the transport a letter to my parents, and told him to post it if anything happened. He handed it back to me after we came out of Trones Wood and I, in some confusion, made a resolve to write no more farewell epistles. But, on the night of the raid, I scribbled again a short note. This time I had a happier idea. I would leave it on the table as an ordinary letter, knowing the post had gone that night and that I could easily retrieve it if I came back.

Half a page of scribbled foolscap and a little rubber doll, this in more than two years was the sum of it; not familiarity but stark necessity had bred contempt. If you were for it, you were for it; it was useless to worry. Some had religion to help them, some were fatalists. And perhaps our instinctive attitude had more in common with the pagan fortitude of Lord Morley's reasoning than with the dark concern of Spencer and Huxley, or the simple trustfulness of the faithful. No fear of something after death, no argued disquiet, no troubled doubts, afflicted us.

But when we were confronted by death, with what light hands we touched the common friend. To a man off his feed Price had offered the mocking counsel: "You had better eat it up, it's as likely as not your last." And to another, down over the death of a pal, "Cheer up, Cockie, it's your turn next." I remember, when bringing in the wounded at

Hooge, I heard a man say "Down you go there, you won't trouble any more to-night," and with that the fellow heaved a dead man into a big crater. It may be that for some this can only be a gruesome glimpse into the dark places of war where some fiend for ever lurks, calling to the savage that is in us all. But for others who can follow the unconscious working of that man's mind, who had orders to bury men dead for days, it becomes a natural mental state evolved to meet a most unnatural contingency. We simply could not afford to allow death to hover in the offing as the final mystery; it must be brought to earth and robbed of its disturbing influence, by rough gibes and the touch of ridicule. If it was firmly grasped like a nettle soon there was no sting left in it.

As the odds shortened, and it became plain that death was to be the common lot, I thought less of its coming until at last I saw no cruelty in its approach. Surely it is a fine free setting forth, this end in the field. It comes to a man in the spring time, before age and disease have soiled his body and the traffic of cities has stained his soul. He has lived his brief manhood among men, knowing what is best in them, and has gone out untouched and undefeated by the petty strife of a world at peace.

"The bird, however hard the frost may be, flies briskly to its customary roosting place, and, with beak tucked into its wing falls asleep . . . and at midnight, or in the early morning, it drops from its perch dead. Yesterday he lived and moved, . . . such marvellous certitude in all his motions, as to be able to drop himself plumb down the tallest tree top or out of the void air on to a slender spray, and scarcely cause its leaves to tremble. Now on this morning, he lies stiff and motionless; so easy and swift is the passage from life to death in wild nature."

Chapter Seventeen

Selection

When an army is being trained to fight it must begin by weeding out those whose character or temperament makes them incapable of fighting. Ideally such men would be rejected by a recruiting board before they became part of the Service. If that is found to be impossible the army must fall back on daily observation of the recruit during his training to detect signs of instability. If both fail to expose the latent weakness of the young soldier it is left to war itself to strip the mask from the man of straw, which it will do with a quite ruthless precision of its own.

What have the recruiting boards been asked to do? When Bacon wrote of the *Strength of Armies* his principle in selecting men had its roots in the virtues of the yokel soldier; it was a physical appraisement. But in the modern world war has become the business of millions, willing and unwilling; the tape measure is not enough. Courage is no longer the product of a vacant mind, it is the expression on the battlefield of character. Can a board in a brief interview with a recruit recognise character? A great industrialist once said to me "I know when a man enters the door if he is my man." There are, I am sure, men who can detect something wrong in a man when he has hardly spoken, as others are sensitive to a false note in music. They possess a gift for selecting the right men for a particular post, a gift that is acknowledged to be half the secret of success in war as it is of most of the achievements of peace. But they are too few to count in any working scheme; they do not sit on recruiting boards. It is not therefore a matter for surprise that these boards have not been very successful in weeding out the misfits of war. They have no clear cut picture in their minds of the man who is not designed by nature to weather the storm of war; they do not venture even on a rough estimate of character; they are content with physical measurements.

When these tests were passed boards have been satisfied hitherto to shut out madmen. The unstable whom they passed as fit to bear arms became a tax on transport and on hospital accommodation; apart from the moral effect they had on others, they squandered the doctors' time. They were returned to civil life a burden to themselves and to the country. More than two years after the Armistice nearly sixty-five thousand men discharged from the army were drawing pensions for neurasthenia. Nor have we yet learnt the lesson. In 1941 twenty thousand soldiers were invalided out of the army for the same reason. We have still to put recruiting on a modern basis and not on a footing invented by Frederick the Great or somebody who measured Grenadiers by the yard.

What may be reasonably asked of such a tribunal? No board in the few moments at its disposal can hope to fathom the character of a recruit, but it should be able to detect in him the signs and symptoms of nervous instability. Such a man may, for example, lack moral sense, without which no soldier can long endure the stress and terror of the modern battlefield. His conduct sheet often betrays him and this document ought to be in the hands of the Board. It is primarily because we have no testaments of that kind that our task is so difficult, for when the past is the surest guide to the future we cannot turn to it for guidance, whereas the Germans have records of their soldiers from childhood. It is more common to find the recruit "simple". An intelligence test applied to all recruits would eliminate those whose minds have not developed—who form perhaps a majority of those we wish to exclude from the army.

It is a modest programme, but it is at least a beginning. To leave it there satisfies no one. Here and there a man is found with a gift for the measurement of men, but his methods evade definition; his tests are subjective, they cannot be taught to others. There is therefore a search for objective evidence of a recruit's intelligence, of the task for which he is most suited and perhaps of his temperament and capacity to remain calm under stress. Tests have been devised and their value is just now much debated. Within their limits they seem to serve a useful purpose. It is true that we have as yet no test of pugnacity, no test of leadership, no test of temperament. We have found no short cuts to such knowledge. For this we must still rely on individual judgment. It is difficult too to check the value of such tests as we have; our conclusions must be tentative until they are proved in battle. At present that proof is often wanting. But if these tests do not help to pick aces, they do help us to get rid of men who will not make soldiers, in particular they detect before he has an accident the pilot who is not fit for the job. The value of tests that seek to sift men according to their aptitude for some particular duty are less firmly established than tests of intelligence, but some at least are worth a trial.

The Germans, who were the first to use tests, are now cautious in their interpretation. Their methods of selection are dominated by a search for character and by a deep laid conviction that no conclusion of any kind has much value until it is put to the test of service in the field. After the tests had been introduced into the German army, Von Seeckt came out against them. A leader, he admitted, must be a good judge of men, if he is not he will fail, but it was all a matter of common sense: and after all Napoleon without tests was the greatest psychologist of all time. Von Seeckt quoted Frederick the Great, "You must die stalwartly". Was there much more to be said? He was answered in 1935 by an anonymous writer who held that young officers must be taught to regard soldiers as individuals with minds of their own.

The exclusion of these misfits is so vital to the peace of mind of armies that I shall make a brief scrutiny of selection practised for that purpose in England and America. The recruiting methods of the British Army before 1914 have been quoted as a triumphant example of successful selection. The outcome of many years experience, they were said to be responsible for an army which the Germans themselves had dubbed "a perfect thing apart". But it was perhaps less simple than that. Apart from the exclusion of men with gross physical deficiencies and an attempt, frequently abandoned, to maintain certain physical standards, selection seems hardly to have been practised. The recruiting sergeant was content if the fish he hooked was in fair condition and a decent weight. Even these modest demands were not always met. The army had to take what it could get; it was dependent on the state of the labour market, relying on the assumption that every year roughly thirty thousand men who were unable to find work in civil life would be willing to enlist; the real recruiting sergeant was unemployment. When trade was good it was often difficult to find enough men for the army; in these conditions young lads of poor upbringing and physique were accepted in the hope that with good food and physical training they would develop into "fit" men in a year or two.

If however I am ready to discount selection by a recruiting sergeant as the explanation of the virtue of that army, I shall accept what I call "natural selection" as one of the two prime factors in the building up of that unusual efficiency. I was satisfied by my years with a battalion in France that there is a breed of men who do not seem to fit into the structure of society; these men are vaguely discontented with the vast inhuman life of cities, its prudent, punctual existence, with its money saving, its daily stress on the need of security; they find in the army at least an alternative to the prison life of great towns. "All warlike people are a little idle, and love danger better than travail." Bacon's words might have been written of the cockney soldiers with whom I served; they would run any risk to save themselves trouble, they would climb out of a water-logged trench fifty yards from the Boche to avoid wading through water; they never appeared to think of danger. We are reminded of the existence of men of this stock when someone throws up his job and goes off to the Pole or sets out to climb some peak in the distant Himalayas, but that a battalion could be made of such people had occurred to no one. The cockney soldier has become a legend, it has been said by more careful folk that the quickness and shrewdness of the non-commissioned officers is the simple explanation of that legend. I doubt whether that is the whole story. If from eight million citizens of London only a few regiments are recruited it is just possible that the rolling stones drifting into them may be enough at any rate to give a character of its own to a London regiment. The life in the army which attracts this breed of men seems to repel the sensitive, emotional, unstable type; I call this natural selection.

I have wandered into a field where it is easy to make large assumptions foreign to my training. It has been roundly affirmed that these men enlisted because they were either unemployed or unemployable. This may be the truth, but it is not the whole truth. That no place can be found in the scheme of things for these lads who when tried in the hell of war did not fail in fortitude, but were guided in their short day by pity, by toleration and by a simple unselfishness—the graces of civilisation—amounts, as I see it, to an indictment of our social architecture.

There are other grounds for my reluctance to use the quality of the British Expeditionary Force of 1914—a matchless army—as an example of what can be done by selection. Though I shall maintain that good soldiers are not bred from bad stock, I do not doubt that many unpromising specimens were transformed by training; in particular by that part of training which consists in inculcating *esprit de corps*. I remember men recruited at the street corner by starvation who came to act on the principle that if the Regiment lived it did not matter if they died, though they did not put it that way. This was their source of strength, their abiding faith, it was the last of all the creeds that in historical times have steeled men against death.

I must return from this digression to trace the history of selection in the last war. On the outbreak of hostilities in 1914, those who had been responsible for recruiting in time of peace were recalled to their Regiments; doctors were asked to pass as many as two hundred recruits in a single day, so that their examination was perfunctory or worse; the machinery collapsed, there was chaos. Even when conscription had been introduced no heed was paid to the recruiting arrangements in countries such as France where conscript armies had long existed. It was not until the final year of the war that any serious attempt was made to discriminate between recruits who were, and those who were not, of normal nervous stability.

In America this tale of ineptitude with its deep stirring of the public conscience had been noted; there was a fixed purpose to do better. A young nation priding itself on its business methods could not tolerate such muddle, such waste. Intelligence tests were applied to nearly two million recruits. The term is perhaps a little misleading. Those who were responsible for the examination, a perfunctory affair lasting ten to fifteen minutes—were poorly equipped for that purpose. Further, even when instability was recognised, the board commonly took no action. There was manifest scepticism as to the value of such new-fangled tests and active antagonism to any examination of this kind. The medical officers were the chief passive obstacles, as they had been in England; they were, according to the War Office report of 1922, slower to recognise the value of military psychology than the combatant officers; they could not bring themselves to believe that a training which transformed poor physical specimens into robust fighting men could fail with recruits whose only trouble was some bother with their minds, a nervous or mental disability. The combatant officers were in the main hardly more sympathetic; they would maintain that if the specialists did not stop eliminating the unfit there would soon be no army left; the introduction of special examinations of so many kinds threatened too to interfere with established military routine. Besides, as "the men looked all right they probably were all right"; after all war was war. The recantation of the Americans when it came was complete, but the change of heart came too late; the project for a scientific examination of recruits launched with such hopes had been destroyed by man's inveterate dislike of the novel in thought or action. No conclusion of any value can be drawn from that vast experiment. Yet I do not think we can accept that failure as final; the price is too high.

Can courage be judged apart from danger? When I first asked that question in France in 1914, there was an air of novelty about the contention that courage is a quality that can be judged apart from danger, quietly and without haste, perhaps in some sleepy hamlet miles from the track of the man of action. It took us by surprise because in England, before 1914, men had ceased to think of war as a thing that might happen to themselves. It had become too remote, too improbable. Any thought of soldiering had been left behind them with their wooden swords and paper caps and boyish images. So those confident dreams of childhood had never been replaced by the trembling curiosity of man, the potential combatant, questioning how he might fare in the heat of battle. He did not plague himself with the dread fear of fear, he did not ask on what courage depends, what courage is, nor even if those around him were men without fear. In 1914, apart from William James' analysis of fear, there was no book in the English tongue on the psychology of the soldier. Men were not interested in the psychology of courage and fear. Wells, in his *Research Magnificent*, had to go to the jungle to illustrate fear—the fear of animals. Even now, after the lapse of a quarter of a century, and in the midst of another war, when we ask whether it is possible to say in time of peace how the men about us will acquit themselves in war, we must answer without much help from any science of the mind. This book of mine might have been written by a soldier without a doctor's training.

It is true that the central purpose of Trotter's book on the Herd Instinct was to suggest that psychology could be, if we would only use it, a guide in the actual affairs of life; it would enable us to understand the human mind sufficiently to foretell in some measure the course of human behaviour. Yet when we have read all he has to say, we are driven to the conclusion that a practical psychology is as yet in its infancy, so selection is still wholly dependent on a knowledge of the real ingredients of courage—what courage is—and an exact appraisement of the degree in which those ingredients are present in the man concerned.

Can courage be judged apart from danger? Can we say, while there is yet peace, of those about us that if war came they would acquit themselves as men?

I may as well admit at the outset that there are some who have little faith in any such sifting process. They will say that men must be put to the crucial test of war before labels are attached to them. War, they affirm, has a way of discovering the true nature of a man; it pays scant attention to the standards of peace, which they assume are different from those of war.

It is altogether a most comfortable doctrine. They would have the best of both worlds. They believe that while there is yet peace a man must do the best for himself; it is the only rational thing to do. He must live for himself, his standards are naturally self and mammon. Suddenly there is war and as suddenly human nature is transfigured. The stir and fervour and exhilaration of the social atmosphere in times of excitement bring out qualities which in peace are dormant. They would imply, those sleek citizens, that beneath a coat of selfishness in peace lay all the qualities we have learnt to prize in war. As practical men, too, they find little profit in these vague speculations about the springs of human conduct. They have not thought of courage as self-discipline, a moral quality.

It is a grey world these clever people live in; they see in human nature only its frailty. These little servants of routine, these poor spirits whose hearts are with their bankers, who sought safety in life and still seek it in the turmoil of a bloody strife, can they impart the secret of constancy in war? "All warlike people are a little idle and love danger better than travail." That love of danger has the ring of another day, but it is still true that the pick of men, as we knew them in the trenches, were not always the chosen of more settled times. These clever people when it came to the choice between life and death called vainly to their gods, they helped them not at all. Success, which in their lives had meant selfishness, had come in war to mean unselfishness. If we once believe that the capacity to get on in life is not everything, we shall be in a fair way to employ in peace tests of character as searching as those which the trenches supplied in war.

I contend that fortitude in war has its roots in morality; that selection is a search for character, and that war itself is but one more test—the supreme and final test if you will

—of character. Courage can be judged apart from danger only if the social significance and meaning of courage is known to us, namely that a man of character in peace becomes a man of courage in war. He cannot be selfish in peace and yet be unselfish in war. Character as Aristotle taught is a habit, the daily choice of right instead of wrong; it is a moral quality which grows to maturity in peace and is not suddenly developed on the outbreak of war. For war, in spite of much that we have heard to the contrary, has no power to transform, it merely exaggerates the good and evil that are in us, till it is plain for all to read; it cannot change, it exposes. Man's fate in battle is worked out before war begins. For his acts in war are dictated not by courage, nor by fear, but by conscience, of which war is the final test. The man whose quick conscience is the secret of his success in battle has the same clear cut feelings about right and wrong before war makes them obvious to all. If you know a man in peace, you know him in war. "The thing a man does practically believe—if you tell me what that is, you tell me to a very great extent what the man is, what the kind of thing he will do is."

If we throw up our hands and confess it is not possible to separate the intrepid soul from the inconstant mob, then the men of an Arctic expedition might be chosen at random. Selection can be done, for it has been done; the only doubt is on what scale it can be practised.

I have stressed the underlying discord between these two views of the anatomy of courage, because if courage has no social significance this book has little meaning, and because this discord is an obstacle to that national unity which has been our strength in war. In the democracies of to-day men will only fight from some overwhelming necessity to protect the moral foundations of their lives and those of their children. Men so charged with feeling recoil instinctively from the material view of life held by a small section of society whose influence exceeds its deserts. The resumption of power by that section after the last war completed the dis-illusionment of men returning from France who are the fathers of the militia to-day.

Six months after the Armistice I wrote:

The clear, war-given insight into the essence of a man has already grown dim. With the coming of peace we have gone back to those comfortable doctrines that some had thought war had killed. Cleverness has come into its own again. The men who won the war never left England; that was where really clever people were most useful. I sometimes wonder what some of those good souls who came through make of it all. They remember that in the life of the trenches a few simple demands were made of all men; if they were not met the defaulter became an outlaw. Do they ask of themselves when they meet the successful of the present how such men would have fared in that other time where success in life had seemed a mirage? Are they silently in their hearts making those measurements of men which they learnt when there was work afoot that was a man's work? They know a man, for reasons which they are too inarticulate to explain, and they are baffled because others deny what seems to them so simple and so sure.

Chapter Eighteen

Discipline

Health and discipline, that is how soldiers have been made through history. The discipline of the English Army in the early days of the Peninsular War was modelled on the methods of Frederick the Great. It was control from without in its crudest, most brutal shape; men did their job because the fear of flogging was greater than the fear of death. Sir John Moore, though he had to handle men of whom Wellington had said "they were the biggest scamps unhung", swept away Frederick's influence, creating in the camp at Shorncliffe a nursery which maintained a steady supply of leaders to Wellington. He left a creed in which the English Army still believes, a creed supported by a faith in human nature. He insisted that the men should be treated as human beings. The officers must know their men, be their friend and look after their wants; even orders were to be given in the language of moderation. It was a discipline of kindness, an appeal to the heart inspired by mutual respect, affection, and comradeship. Officers learnt to prevent crime by winning the affection of their men. Control from without had been replaced by control from within. When I compare the discipline of persuasion and the discipline of punishment I shall not say that one is right and the other wrong, only that the discipline of punishment is out of place in the national armies of to-day.

The discipline of our national armies is very different from that of Frederick's day. Corporal punishment has vanished from the Army and the Navy, speaking broadly it has vanished from our prisons. There have, of course, been relapses. It is unlikely that Frederick's brutal and arbitrary conception of the management of men will ever be completely exorcised from the human mind. Small Fredericks from time to time will strut the stage, since power has an erosive quality even more penetrating than fear. There is, however, no reason to believe that soldiers are more given to the abuse of power than any other section of the community. If Frederick's ideas are not dead in the English Army, they are at any rate moribund. From the German Army, which maintains no guardhouses, they have been completely extirpated. That one soldier should watch over another with a gun is repugnant to the German military ideal. If a soldier commits a criminal offence which requires his imprisonment he has no right to remain a soldier. Nor can his fellow soldiers be asked to associate with a criminal. The offender is handed over to the civilian authorities; he is summarily and dishonourably discharged from the army to which he can never return. Even for minor offences no degrading penalties are imposed; punishment, we are told, has no longer a place in their army.

The discipline of our army of to-day—I am concerned only with the form of discipline most suitable for a nation in arms—is open to criticism of another kind. Everywhere men are asking whether a system of discipline and training designed for the illiterate has been modified to meet the needs of an educated rank and file. They agree that discipline is necessary, but hold that it should be a means to an end and not an end in itself. They complain that the soldier's conception of discipline has hardly altered as men's minds have changed. It is still a discipline of the body and not of the mind, the perfect and polished co-ordination of certain formal movements. They ask—and they are open to correction—if a certain relaxation of discipline is necessarily injurious to the efficiency of an army.

Before I try to find an answer to that question I want to say a word on freedom of speech. Once when I had given a lecture at the Staff College at Camberley, the Commandant introduced me to his brother officer commanding Sandhurst, and it was arranged that I should give the same lecture to his cadets at some future date. But when the Commandant had slept on it he changed his mind: my views on discipline in particular were strong wine for these lads who were only nineteen. The wine must be watered. The lecture was never given. In any other profession men of that age would be at Oxford or Cambridge listening to the whole gamut of opinion. But we must take heed when men ask whether senior officers can maintain discipline if their juniors are critical and outspoken. This freedom of speech, I am told, might undermine the authority of senior officers by making them appear incompetent. If it did I should have no more to say, for I admit at once that to put any plan into practice obedience must be automatic; the junior officer must carry out the orders of his seniors, right or wrong. But is the authority of senior officers so precariously balanced in these days? For twenty years I have been responsible for the discipline of four hundred medical students of much the same age. If one can meet their criticisms and answer their questions, with perhaps a little in hand, if one can give a reason for everything discipline is not destroyed, though it may be partly replaced by leadership.

If criticism is the oxygen without which the mind of youth cannot grow, is this the only respect in which it is possible to relax discipline without impairing the efficiency of the machine? Consider the discipline of the pilots and of the submarine service of this war, and that of the Australians of the last war.

The pilots' discipline in flying in formation is as strict as any. They know that it is reasonable and necessary, that without it the flight would find trouble. But once they have landed it is another story. They will not submit, I am told, to a stringent discipline such as the Guards accept. Bader, who lost both legs in an accident before the war, had become a legend before he had to bale out. One day, shortly before his capture, the officer at the head of the Fighter Command, while visiting Bader's station said he would like to talk to him, but when they came to tell Bader, he said shortly that he didn't want to see him. These pilots are kittle cattle, they need careful handling. They have deliberately chosen a particularly risky job. They have learnt by experience that they can see it through without much control from without, that discipline in this sense is unnecessary, because it has been replaced by a sound morale, control from within.

The prestige of the submarine service is high in the Navy. Before the war officers and men volunteered for this branch of the service, the hazards of the life attracted them. No one below the rank of Able Seaman was taken, and the record of that seaman must have been without blemish: if one of this picked body of men fell short of the demands the Service makes, he was at once sent back to the more humdrum existence of a surface ship. The discipline at sea is paternal; the officers in grey flannels and sweaters know all about their men and their families, while the men are not in doubt that the officers know their job, they will go anywhere for them. The inspection and saluting business hardly exist. Back in harbour the crew go to a depot ship, and once more ordinary discipline is the rule. With various crews gathered into one ship the family party has been broken up and a different kind of control is again necessary. Discipline can be relaxed at sea because the men are exceptional; their fine spirit makes everything possible. "If you get results, the less discipline the better," one of their officers said to me.

The Australians of the last war were magnificent fighting stock, but for discipline in the sense in which we use that term they cared nothing. They had lived on their sheep farms close to nature; it was no life for the soft. An independent spirit was native to them; they were on good terms with themselves. In them was planted a rugged strain of obstinacy that war awoke. Once they had got their teeth into a task they would not let go. Once more, they could not believe that discipline as we understand that term was necessary. They got on quite well in battle without it.

A man under discipline does things at the instigation of someone in authority, and if he doesn't he is punished. A man with a high morale does things because in his own mind he has decided to do them without any suggestion from outside sources. Discipline, control from without, can only be relaxed safely when it is replaced by something higher and better, control from within. To put it differently, discipline loses much of its vital importance when the human material—officers and men—is exceptional. Men rebel against discipline when they know in their hearts that it is not necessary. This they can only know with any assurance in the presence of danger, which is the acid test of their morale. It is therefore not wise to tamper with discipline in any way when men are not in danger; it can only be relaxed with impunity as a spontaneous act of some hard fighting unit in whose experience the more rigid forms of discipline have been found to be superfluous. If discipline is relaxed when it has not been replaced by a high morale, you get a mob who will obey their own primitive instincts like animals. For the soldiers in England, who are suffering from years of inaction and boredom, more not less discipline is necessary.

The relaxation of discipline in a submarine is not of course thought out—it just happens. As far as it has an ancestry it is a manifestation in war of something which at present does not amount in England to more than a deep distrust of coercive measures. This in turn has grown out of the spirit of toleration of the English people, who for centuries have lived free from fear of their neighbours. It is the temper of an English army on active service, so surprising and so attractive in its detachment and freedom from passion.

There is nothing revolutionary in this conception of discipline. I do not question that it is essential to the control of armies, but I do affirm that its influence on the soldier's mind has been exaggerated. And this distrust of coercive measures has been strengthened by experience in war. Officers in France, the pick of them, seemed instinctively to realise, as time passed, that to get the best results out of their men they must appeal to the best that was in them. The crack of the whip was of no avail.

This discipline of kindness has won converts in strange places. Von der Goltz, speaking for the Germans, asks if a martinet has ever made a good soldier on active service. His whole thoughts are absorbed in the minutiae of discipline; his ideas soar no higher than pipeclay and buttons. He tells us that the secret of the strength of the German Army is to be found in the interest the officers take in their men. But others of his race were not so sure, they had become aware in the war of the gap which yawned between officers and men in their Army, a gap which was closed when they were bundled off together to a labour camp for six months. That began about the time when the slogan "Back to 1914", with its implied elimination of the rankers who had won commissions during the war, went round the regimental messes of our regular army. Prussian discipline had become a pattern of severity. We sometimes forget they have been sensible enough to see that it doesn't always work. The instructions which their High Command issues to officers to guide their relations with their men are undiluted Moore.

I do not pretend that everyone in our Army is equally enlightened. If there are some who have no faith in measures of coercion, holding that whatever disappointments may await us we must put our trust in human nature, there are others who in their hearts admit no more than that flogging is no longer expedient. There is a cleavage of opinion, I think, because some soldiers when confronted by difficulties in the management of men can see only man in the mass, while others are instinctively dealing with individuals, with whose trials and hopes they are in sympathy. Man is made one way or the other. When Octavia Hill, at the age of fourteen, was put in charge of a workroom of rough and undisciplined school children, she began by tearing down from the wall a list of punishments invented by her predecessor. She was able to do this because she did not regard the children as a class, but simply as Louisa and Clara and Elizabeth.

I gave this chapter to General Marshall to read. "This", he said, "is written for the professional soldier. Go away and tackle the disciplining of the citizen soldier. That is the problem of this war." This citizen soldier conforms to no single type; in a national army there are many who will only respond to the rigid discipline of the past, but there are others who find this hourly bludgeoning irksome. They must have a reason for what they do. They are alert, but they are casual; they are quick to see that an order could be carried out in another and more sensible way, but they awake only slowly to the consequences if orders are not obeyed to the letter.

In a certain bombing raid the plan was to drop all the bombs in sixty seconds. A pilot in command of a section of the great fleet of aircraft calculated that he would not be spotted so soon by radio-location if he flew at a lower altitude. So he took his command down below the rest of the bombers. But at this height aircraft cannot fly at the same speed so that he arrived at the target forty minutes after the rest of the flight had dropped their bombs. Some of these had a delayed action and they contributed to the inferno into which he led his bombers.

What is the remedy? If the men are devoted to their officers the problem vanishes. But often an officer who had won popularity before coming under fire by his leniency and softness in letting his men down too lightly loses their regard under fire, while the officer who had been unpopular under peace conditions on account of his severity comes into his own. Robert E. Lee, a tolerant man, believed in the death penalty. In the American army all men before joining a special branch of the service have to submit to three months basic training when the soldier learns the necessity of doing exactly and precisely what he is told to do—for this is the crux of the matter.

At this stage the Brigade of Guards is generally paraded for the confusion of the critic. It is a simple argument: the Guards, they say, were the most efficient unit in France in the last war and that efficiency was due to discipline. Therefore all that is needed is more and more discipline. There are, of course, two assumptions in that argument. Since the various units of the Army in France were never submitted to any common test, it is perhaps rash to speak of any unit as the best. There is, in fact, reason to believe that in the retreat from Mons the Guards were in no way exceptional in the Regular Army, which was a "perfect thing apart". Again the efficiency of the Guards later in the war—and it is not in dispute—was due to factors other than discipline. They were a privileged body. No half trained recruits were sent to their trenches; every man passed through a strict training in the depot before being sent to France. Further, as the war dragged on and human material deteriorated, companies in the line were perturbed when a proved and seasoned soldier was hit; they knew that when he was fit he would be sent to another unit and that his place might be taken by some raw conscript. When on the other hand the wounds of a man in the Guards were healed he went back to the Guards. It would not be difficult to pile up evidence that the efficiency of the Guards was due to other factors than discipline. Nevertheless apart from their fine record, the influence and prestige of the Guards in the regular army are such that it is worth while to enquire how they think discipline works.

Lord Gort, who commanded a battalion of the Grenadier Guards in France in 1917, has given us his own conception —"In peace training the great thing is drill. No doubt you want something to help you over your fears and if you get control of the nerves, as you do in drill, it helps largely, and it helps to drive the man forward in war . . . the feeling of unionism—of moving together—is a great help, and this is brought out by the soldiers' training—drill."

It is not easy of course to disentangle in a good battalion what is due to the mutual confidence of professional soldiers, that gives them a sense of security which the Greeks believed was the first source of strength in war, from what may be ascribed to *esprit de corps* and devotion to the regiment. But is this really the purpose of training in a modern army? I wonder, does a man learn self-control by drill after joining the Army? This seems to me scarcely to do justice to Lord Gort, a soldier of character. I see no reason to believe that at the present day men can be reconciled to premature death by sloping arms daily for many months, and I am sometimes puzzled why the Guards put so much faith in precision of movement, so little in precision of thought. They seem to think that men should repeat certain actions until they become automatic, when at a crisis habit will save them from falling under the sway of their primitive instincts. A man's mind is to be grooved as a golf-swing is grooved by the same movements constantly repeated; he becomes an automaton.

I remember—it is strange how, as we grow older, we can only recall batting on good wickets and making runs—once advancing criticism of this kind to a military audience in which the Brigade of Guards was strongly represented, and how they rose against the blasphemy. Outnumbered and pressed on all sides, I found refuge in the story of an experiment in physiology taken from my student days. A nail was thrust into a frog's head so that its brain was destroyed and it felt nothing. But the frog continued to make the same movements as before. "I do not, gentlemen, suggest an analogy . . ." What a mouth of answering laughter drowned the rest of the sentence, covering my retreat! Men who can take criticism of all they cherish most in that spirit leave the critic humble, but assured that the Brigade of Guards will presently become a model to the national, as it has been to the professional, army.

Discipline can form a habit and the force of habit is regal. But does this theory of discipline explain why men are ready to die in battle? The difference between a battalion of the professional army of 1914 and a Kitchener unit was not that years of training had made the actions of the regular soldier automatic, but that they had implanted in the very marrow of the men the creed of the Regiment which blossomed into a living faith till nothing else mattered. Who shall say how much of the efficiency of the Guards is due to discipline and how much to devotion to the Brigade? The secret of morale is not a negative quality, the insulation of a man's mind from disturbing impressions. It is a positive virtue, a motive for altruism.

What England owes to the Brigade of Guards is something more subtle than the part they have played in her professional army in peace by setting standards of precision in the technique of drill for all to imitate, and in war by exacting from officers and men alike a tacit agreement, that the only way to leave their trenches was on a stretcher. We are beginning to understand that the secret of the awful power of the German army is not in tanks and aircraft, but in a certain attitude of mind of her manhood: a pride in arms, in being permitted to join the sacred fellowship of military men, a pride in being chosen a soldier of the fatherland. The German soldier is considered by himself and by the nation a member of a privileged brotherhood, his military training gives him a feeling of superiority. Every man in the Guards has the same feeling, but he only makes obeisance to the Brigade of Guards, from the rest of the army he dissociates himself, even his buttons are sewn to his tunic in a distinctive fashion, whereas the German soldier accepts the whole army as his brotherhood.

This pride in arms is usually associated with polished buttons, erect carriage and things of that kind, but these are not cause but effect. No doubt we have erred in our neglect of symbols, the outward and visible manifestations of inner loyalties, but it is not the absence of military bands from the streets and all the pomp and circumstance of war which we miss. It is the attitude of the nation to its army that is at fault. Is the citizen full of pride and hot loyalty when he joins the army? Does it give him prestige among his fellow countrymen to be seen in uniform? The answers to those questions may determine victory. If we must answer no, we are sending our citizen army limping into battle. There are folk who win easy laughter by guying types which are largely extinct. "If they make an Aunt Sally of our army they will get an Aunt Sally army." That was the warning given to me by one of our most successful soldiers. When the Prime Minister visited the army not long ago a battalion of the Coldstream was paraded before him; as he watched the perfect rhythm of their movements his eyes filled with tears. Only those who have got to the heart of this business of making soldiers can understand that surge of feeling, can feel what he felt.

This pride in arms—it is a bad name for in our army it is a much more domestic feeling like the affection of a crew for their ship—was of course an abiding source of strength in the regular army during the early part of the last war. But it never took root in the citizen force upon which the brunt of the struggle fell later. This I believe to be the contribution the Guards have made to training men—Guardsmen—for war. But I want them to help the army to move with the times. When I used to talk on these matters to soldiers before the war I found them very ready to listen to a subject which had had no place in their training until then. The Staff College and the Sappers caught up my points as professional actors take their cues, the various commands made my task easy, but in the London Command I had a feeling that I was shouting at the closed mind of a conscripted audience of Guards subalterns. It was not necessary to talk to the Guards about morale and the rest of the army was not their concern. If the Guards are to be set up as a model to a nation in arms, they must submit to the creed that there is another discipline besides the discipline of movement—the self-discipline that drives a man to the mastery of his art through long laborious days, eschewing pleasure.

Chapter Nineteen

The support of numbers

It is difficult to sustain the soldier's spirit in a lonely out-post; he is conscious of a sense of isolation. Between him and the main unit living further back in comparative security and comfort a gulf opens. His own fate is always in his mind; he begins to have a fellow feeling for the soldier in enemy outposts. In the Western Desert where

> "Boundless and bare
> The lone and level sands stretch far away,"

the crew of a tank or armoured car, seemingly deserted, are left with their own thoughts.

When the name shell-shock was coined the number of men leaving the trenches with no bodily wound leapt up. The pressure of opinion in the battalion—the idea stronger than fear—was eased by giving fear a respectable name. When the social slur was removed and the military risks were abolished the weaklings may have decided in cold blood to malinger, or perhaps when an alternative was held out the suggestion of safety was too much for their feeble will. The resolve to stay with the battalion had been weak·

ened, the conscience was relaxed, the path out of danger was made easy. The hospitals at the base were said to be choked with these people though the doctors could find nothing wrong with them. Men in France were weary. Unable or unwilling? It was no longer a private anxiety, it had become a public menace.

Soldiers in France in 1917 and 1918 had more need of the support of the corporate opinion of their units in the face of danger—the support of numbers—than those who had fought up to the battle of the Somme. The history of the use of mustard gas by the Germans brings out that need by warning us—with the emphasis of figures—what may befall an army which has forgotten that a soldier's conduct is shaped by what is expected of him. First used in July, 1917, there were one hundred and thirteen thousand casualties from this gas; it was a bid for a decision. At one time it appeared that it might come to play on land the part the submarine filled at sea.

Late in 1917 I was sent to Boulogne to find some means of checking the backward stream. In a quarter of these men we found a nervous disorder—frequently hysteria—implanted on the physical harm caused by the gas, which in itself was often trivial. When after a few days the bodily hurt had gone, there was left an emotional disturbance like a mild attack of shell shock. The physical effects were often absent or of no moment; it was the mind that had suffered hurt. Mustard gas, after July, 1917, partly usurped the role of high explosive in bringing to a head a natural unfitness for war, or less commonly in undermining a fitness sapped by exceptional stress in the field.

In making a point that has been overlooked it would be easy to stretch the truth. Mustard gas was the cause of grave physical injury: of every hundred gassed men, thirteen had to be sent to England. But the majority were more frightened than hurt.

A soldier of judgment wrote to me: "during a gas attack

a hundred and fifty men drifted away from the battalion on our right while only ten left the Fusiliers, though the conditions were the same." Could those fellows have stayed if they had wished? Was it the presence of gas or the absence of discipline?

It was true of most of these men, as it was of the soldier mildly shocked by shell fire, that once they were allowed to leave the neighbourhood of the line for some base hospital, their career as soldiers was at an end; only the support of opinion in their own battalions could save them. The doctors behind the line had missed the true meaning of this glut of gassed men; their failure weakened the purpose of the army in France when it most needed strengthening. These men were mishandled, consequently it is difficult to measure the value of mustard gas as a weapon of warfare. Since the mortality proved to be only two in a hundred, the effectiveness of the gas depended on the number gassed, their loss of confidence and the average length of time a gassed man was away from the line. We proceeded to ascertain by the crucial test of experience the precise length of time that elapsed before each individual soldier could march in his equipment half a mile to a convalescent camp. Of every hundred men who reached the base, eighty-seven successfully passed that test within a month of gassing; once more the emphasis fell on the trivial character of the physical injury done to many of the men by mustard gas. This army of gassed men, more than a hundred thousand strong, with their disorders of the mind, was at the bottom an expression of trench fatigue. These vapours had set them free from the bondage of the line, for which they were not designed by nature; they could satisfy at last their yearning for security without exciting the open disapproval of their fellows. This was only one more act in the drawn out drama of their soldiering.

Gas becomes a menace when the manhood of a nation has been picked over. Men who have lost or have never had the will to meet the shocks of war sleep lightly when they are half listening for the Strombos horn to summon them to face a gas attack. They dream that they are choking, they smell fumes which have strange and deadly consequences. And when at last death comes down the wind a blinding fear of the unknown seizes upon them and may destroy them. Then if the bracing support of battalion opinion has been allowed to sag, the waverer is left at the mercy of his instincts and victory begins to look a long way off, but what I wonder became of pity in those ruthless years?

When I look back I see that I was caught up in the atmosphere of the trenches. It was inevitable and no more than an instinct of self-preservation that the standards necessary to win should not be lowered. Good fellows in the line did not believe in shell-shock, they did not want to believe in it. Perhaps in their hearts, knowing what lay ahead, they could not altogether approve too sensitive men.

I was perturbed at that time not by any difficulty in shaping opinion in the battalion, but by a gnawing anxiety lest the hard temper of the hour should drive men beyond what was fair and just. What was right was also what was expedient, for a sense of injustice eats away the soldier's purpose. Even now after twenty years my own conscience is troubled by the summary judgments passed on some poor wretch in those days, and by my own part in those verdicts.

After I had left France for another Front I find this note in my diary:

> One day in billets not long ago I heard a car stop outside my hut and found a doctor whom I had known in London before the war. He said he had some work to do in these parts and thought I might like a drive; we went off in high spirits. He said he was much fitter out here and liked the life and hoped the war would go on a long time yet, and as for me there was spring in the air and a car was a novelty. He stopped presently outside a casualty clearing station.

"There's a fellow here who ran away from the trenches," he said, "they are going to shoot him and they want me to say if he is responsible. I shan't be long," and with that he disappeared among the huts.

It was very peaceful in the sunshine, but my mind was no longer at rest. These rough decisions worried me because they were not decisions at all but only guesses with a bullet behind one of them. Was that poor devil crouching in that hut, who was to lose his life because he had sought to save it really responsible? Could any man who knew little of war and less of him decide by looking at him?

It is only bad stock that brings defeat. If I could leave it there it would not be difficult, but I am asked to judge men, to label their motives, and if I am wrong they may be shot not by the enemy but by men of their own race. I think often of the men I have sent back to the trenches, when they have told me they could not carry on, that they were done. Were they really unable or only unwilling? If I had made a mistake, and it was easy to make mistakes, if I were wrong, God help some poor soul. The officers used to say with a chuckle that no man can get past the "Doc" to the base without real sickness or a wound, and I wondered if my answer to that question, unable or unwilling, had been coloured by pride that this battalion is an example to all in the shortness of its sick list; if that was all what a paltry self-sufficiency! What consequences!

There was a fellow who was indifferent to bullets but who could not stand shelling, and another who could not keep still in a bombardment but who would walk up and down the trench, though he must have known that he was much safer in a dug-out, and the sergeant at Armentières who shot himself; these men at least were not selfish, they were unable, not unwilling. It is a time of lonely decisions. I cannot complain if no man helps me to find an answer to this riddle of human conduct, which is perhaps insoluble. The more I see of fear the more reluctant I grow to sit in judg-

ment on these poor victims of past time. I thought
again of the sergeant at Armentières. It was plain
enough then that he could not face war and was not
certain what he might do, and had taken the matter
into his own hands before he did something dreadful
that might bring disgrace on himself and on his regiment. Was it right that I should hold such men to the
trenches and if they were killed were they or I to
blame? But in this life the individual shrinks to nothing, he has no longer the right to an opinion, only the
regiment matters.

Chapter Twenty

Leadership

It is not my purpose to write of the intangible quality which we call genius. I am concerned only with certain practical aspects of leadership which affect morale. Leadership in this sense is the capacity to frame plans which will succeed and the faculty of persuading others to carry them out in the face of death. But even in that limited sense I cannot escape from some enquiry, however superficial, into the nature of this capacity to plan. General Wavell—the last of a long line of writers who have sought to isolate the secret of leadership—makes light of this business of framing plans; strategy is simple stuff, the principles of which can be learnt in a very short time by any reasonable intelligence; administration is "the real crux of generalship". General Wavell does not explain why in the First German War when our troops were probably better fed, better clothed, housed and doctored than ever before, there was no generalship in our army in France worth the name. It is pleasant and even reassuring at this hour to find a soldier moving among the writers of antiquity as among friends, but we should be even more in General Wavell's debt if he had given us that explanation.[1]

[1] General Wavell has since explained to me that the war in France was a siege and that this accounts for the apparent paradox.

De Gaulle writing in 1934 invited his readers to discard the habits of thought of the last war; the continuity of fronts, the long delay before a battle while preparations were being made, the impossibility of developing local successes. He reminded us that five or six times between the spring of 1915 and the autumn of 1918 the French and German armies broke through and a decision seemed to be imminent, but that nothing came of these operations because the infantry found themselves "in the air", lost, footsore and decimated; without guns, without reinforcements and even without orders, so that they could be driven no further. What was lacking to bring victory which had been denied to both armies for so long? De Gaulle answered that question in some detail; he explained how the irruption of an armoured force, men made safe and mobile by tanks, blazing ahead, careless of its flanks, would change everything. Time has given its sanction to his prescient words, though only the Germans listened to him then. It has all happened exactly as he said then that it would happen. The point with which we are here concerned is why this solution to the problem was not found in 1916 or 1917. Were the means not available—the tanks too primitive— or was there no general then in France with the wits to make use of the new machinery? When we ask why Allenby, whose campaign in Palestine was a pattern of its kind, had been no better than the rest in France we seem hot on the track of the nature of this planning gift: the capacity to give birth to new ideas or at any rate to handle them with precision as opposed to the intelligent application of older conceptions.

General Fuller has ascribed the dearth of leaders in those years to the need of a new type of general with the mental outfit to master new forms of warfare. He has drawn a picture of this new captain of war and his professional army —the great engineering College of the nation—led by scientists and officered by fighting engineers; an army of mechanics absorbed in the design of more effective weapons of destruction with their hearts in their workshops and laboratories. Those who remember the battalion officer of 1914, a feudal creature singularly remote from the age of machines, who spoke of sappers indulgently as "mad, methodist or married", can only rub their eyes.

Every forward looking mind thinks his own profession is the most hidebound. If the army is instinctively opposed to change, if it is bound by tradition, that is the way in every walk of life. Radical change is only accepted at the hands of genius or slowly and grudgingly by the sheer pressure of events. Before the discovery of anaesthetics surgery was confined to a few operations carried out at great speed while the victim was forcibly held down; for centuries the barber surgeon was content to cut for stone. Then at a stroke the use of chloroform and ether opened the whole body to the surgeon's knife. Likewise in the soldier's craft after a great stretch of time during which his bible recounted the lessons of history, the campaigns of the great captains, there came the liberating moment when the appearance of the internal combustion engine—comparable to the discovery of anaesthetics—quite altered war.

De Gaulle looked to the customary method of training in the French Army for a partial explanation of their conventional outlook. The endless discourses by well supervised professional lecturers, the innumerable text books, the centralisation of all things "keep every rank in narrow strings". He put no trust in the apprentice system; he believed in education in the broadest sense of the word, in general culture. "At the root of Alexander's victories", he declares, "one will always find Aristotle."

That doctrine has not unduly influenced our choice of leaders. "Haig's interests", according to Buchan, a friendly witness, "were limited. When eminent and cultivated guests came on a visit to G.H.Q., to prevent the Commander-in-Chief sitting tongue tied a kind of conversational menu had to be arranged. For example, Walter Pater, who had been his tutor, had once said something to him about style which he remembered, and it was desirable to lead the talk up to that."

De Gaulle may be right, but most men who think for themselves have little faith in the pedagogue's power to mould others. They agree with Gibbon that the only people we can teach are those who do not need it.

Consider now how the soldier is persuaded to carry out the plans of his leaders.

The art of command is the art of dealing with human nature. The soldier is governed through his heart and not through his head. The complete acceptance in the soldiers' training of that creed with all its implications is the particular contribution England has made to the business of making soldiers. It began, I think, with Moore—it was the foundation of the discipline of his camp at Shorncliffe. The men's response to kindness led them to accept the religion of the Regiment—that only the Regiment matters; a faith which made our professional army before the last war, in German words, "a perfect thing apart". I could illustrate that devotion from almost any page of my diary—

> This morning a man came to me with an abscess in his hand and some fever. Last night there were ten degrees of frost and his hand must have given him hell, throbbing throughout his cold watch, but he would not hear of hospital, he would not even hear of rest. He meant to go back and when I had cut it, back he went.

In bad trenches, when the Boche was active, in the depths of winter with water everywhere, in the sky and in the trench, making life a vile sodden dreary thing it was the unwritten law among the men that they should not go sick.

When we were back in billets it was another story. I knew at once when there were digging parties at night by the number of my visitors. Working parties during rest were not cricket; the rules of the game had been broken. Black sheep there were of course, but the few sick that I saw in the trenches were old friends, they came without hope, they had no reputation to lose, in the Company they were well known. These apart the men would not come near me until they were hit, they no more thought of crossing the door of my dug-out than a respectable tradesman will be seen entering a pawn shop in his own street.

During the battle of the Somme there were no sick. It was the creed of the Regiment, part of their being. Barty Price told me of a man in "A" Company who, returning from leave, was put into the guard room at Dover, drunk, and was sent over by the next boat when sober. On his arrival, finding the battalion in billets, he did not rejoin his Company but went straight to the guard room to report himself. Later he came before the Colonel and told his tale.

"Were you drunk, Smith?"
"Yes, sir," he answered promptly.
The Colonel looked at him for a moment and said, "You've done well, Smith, to get back in time. I shall only admonish you."
"They were children," Barty explained, "and you must treat them as children. He was probably paralytically drunk before he left London but he would not outstay his leave."

A day came when officers of the new army who had not learnt to think as this man came back from leave days late under cover of medical certificates too easily bought.

There was only one religion in the regular army, the regiment; it seemed to draw out of them the best that was in them. In a trench one day I overheard a man explaining away the shortcomings of a temporary officer. "That bloke 'e's only a civvy," he said, just as we speak of one who has never had a chance in life. It was the pride of an old family.

I remember one summer day at Tewkesbury overhearing a man explain to his small son what happened at the battle—"The Lancastrians, that's Uz," he said. And I used to get the same feeling of continuity on the anniversary of Albuera when a sheet of print with Napier's burning tribute to the 7th Foot was given to each of our men, who regarded the incident as quite creditable to their immediate forebears in the Regiment.

How far that appeal to the soldier's heart was reinforced by the personal qualities of his officers could never be measured with any degree of precision. Broadly speaking, it is a question of contact. The Commander-in-chief may be only a name to his army, but a battalion is at the mercy of its officers. When, however, I search the pages of my diary, which is concerned with the personal leadership of platoons. companies, and the battalion itself, for the particular qualities which give to a few dominion over their fellows I can discern only the simplest virtues. Yet these men with their gift of leadership were in the last war the cement strengthening the hastily built edifice of a national army. Now when once more we are searching for youngsters with this gift to command companies and platoons we find that the Air Force has often had first call on adventurous youth. But we dare not admit defeat. So much depends on leadership in a citizen army that I shall not hesitate to break my argument while I attempt to bring to life a few subalterns in my battalion who winning the allegiance of their men kept it to the end.

Anyone who was at Armentières in the early months of the last war will know whom I mean by Mike. He was a little fellow who walked a trifle stooped, with knees always a little bent, in a manner never seen in towns, so that to meet him loping along and hitting the air with a bit of cane sent one back to terriers and rat-infested ditches. Canvas leggings, light-coloured and a little short, so that now and then they showed the tops of his boots, covered legs that knew nothing of fatigue, though they were incredibly thin and rather bandy as if nature had intended that he should live upon a horse. His hat was pulled down until it rested on his ears, pushing them out a little, and came down in front over the smallest, clearest eyes, little beads that shone and danced when he laughed.

Save when a yarn was spun racy and in good humour or the talk was "horse", he heard but half that was said, yet would chime in with an affirmative that he pronounced "yaas" with a slight drawl so that few suspected his inattention. Mike's laugh was worth a week of talk, which was as well, for he was generally content with a sentence at a time. But sometimes he would, a little irrespective of the subject, though always to a suitable circle, drop into a West Country dialect, for he was a clever mimic. All winter he waded through the trenches making hunting sounds and apparently as content with life as he had always been with his ferrets and his dogs in the West Country. Yet he was shrewd, and had a measure of financial talent. This, with some proficiency in the Flemish tongue acquired when a boy, marked him out to settle claims, and the folk of Flanders, grasping and hard, met in him their master.

When the battalion was resting, and officers and men were quartered upon the small houses that fringed the town and make up the suburb of Chapel Armentières, he went almost nightly to the Follies, a Divisional Show, perhaps the first of its kind in France. He would get there early that he might secure a seat close to the stage and when the curtain went up his face screwed up into one long bubble of merriment that sounded not unlike the laughter songs one hears upon the stage. Soon the oldest major of the line began to chuckle and giggle more or less in spite of anything that happened upon the stage, so infectious are original virtues.

One day a gramophone was unearthed from somewhere and when the records arrived it was agreed that

Mike should have the toy. It kept him busy; he would fiddle among the records making hunting sounds till he had found the piece he wanted, and then, as it lilted on, the words in their escape made a little more brazen than their author had designed, he tittered and bubbled into laughter, making little gestures with his arms while his whole body tingled with the tune, now taking a few steps as a ballet girl might, then for a moment exaggerating the movements of the fox-trot till all who saw him were lifted out of that little dreary life back to the days of peace and home.

He filled out and thrived, trudging through the mud, cheerful and quite unaffected by all that makes up war. "Mike," Barty once said when he had looked at him for a long time, "I don't believe the war worries you a bit." He paused at a loss for an answer for he was not given to introspection, and at last said "No" as if it were strange that the question should be put to him at all, and as if he half suspected that they were making fun of him.

One day early in February he was sent into Armentières to bring up a Kitchener detachment that was to be attached to his company for forty-eight hours' instruction. As they came up across the sodden fields towards the trenches, perhaps picturing in the gathering darkness vague bogies of war which they were to meet now for the first time, he went before them switching the air and swinging along in his peculiar way, and when he remembered them from time to time, he turned about and half to them, half to himself, observed "Come along with ye, ye varmints, away now." And then loped on again, thinking perhaps of some great hunt, thinking more probably of nothing at all. For all the restlessness had gone into his muscles and it was apparent that it was just a mistake that he lived in this century at all, who so clearly belonged to a time before great towns, machinery and the reading of books quite altered life.

People had said that the Bluff was taken because

there was no one on the look out during a bombardment : everyone was taking cover and the Boche just
walked over without a shot being fired. Mike must
have heard the yarn, he did not comment upon it, and
I had forgotten all about it till one day when we were
in the Menin Road the Hun began shelling us heavily.
It looked as if he had turned every gun in the salient
on to our trenches and things began to look like business. "It's the goods this time," a Canadian with us
exclaimed. Mike stood on the fire step throughout,
ready to give the signal if the Hun came over. "Hould
that one for me," he cried with a little gurgle of
laughter as they burst all round him.

He always seemed a little strange on foot; when
sports were organised he would get up on any old skin
finishing last with the same happy laugh. He had no
desire to impress anyone with his horsemanship or with
anything else. We learnt to love Mike that winter. The
little fellow had a great heart, he could not think evil
of anyone and none was ever heard to speak a word in
his detraction. He was the last to sit in judgment and
when a man was attacked he quietly came forward in
his defence, giving no reasons, saying simply he liked
"the old thing". I remember when the Colonel had
gone, a lot of us were dilating on his faults, presently
Mike said "I liked old Chang," and he defended another who was held to be supremely stupid saying "I
haven't much brains myself." It was a year before I
learnt that he had likes and dislikes just as the rest of
men.

Everyone knew him and at the tea shop in the town
anyone wearing the Fusilier grenade was sure to be
asked about "Meeshell" by the ministering fairy. That
was Mike of Armentières.

Apart from all the rest, alone in its influence over the
hearts of men I place phlegm—a supreme imperturbability
in the face of death which half amused them and half
dominated them—the ultimate gift in war. During an

attack on Guillemont in the Battle of the Somme an officer of the Rifle Brigade was crossing the open under heavy shell fire when he dropped his glove. He walked back two or three yards, picked it up and went on.

Ypres, September, 1915—

This morning the Boche put over some heavy stuff and there were a good many casualties; all the officers in D Company except Hill were wounded. I was scrambling over a bit of their trench that had been knocked about badly and was more a series of shell holes than a trench, when I met Hill.

As usual he put the thing into perspective at once. "We were very lucky," he said cheerfully, "they haven't done so much damage considering, just this bit of trench happened to get it."

There is something steadying about Hill under these circumstances. He was shaving in the trench. I passed the time of day with him, gave him the gossip from behind and pushed on. He did not tell me that before the show began the Boche had got a direct hit on his dug-out when he was asleep in the far end, and that by some miracle he had been extricated out of a mass of sand bags and fallen supports none the worse. He was not in the least rattled. "He is a wonderful old thing," my informant chuckled, "nothing fizzes on him." Hill is the sort of man you do not get to know in a hurry, it was months before I discovered him. Of course I used to run into him at times, in the trenches by Porte Egale farm, before Armentières, where he lived with his platoon, and he would say "Good morning, Doc," but in the sort of way you speak to a man in another regiment. He seemed to say "I don't know anything about you and I am not particularly anxious to go out of my way to find out," he said it in a perfectly civil and almost friendly fashion. But you would not call him reserved, he is the type of Briton who wants to know whether a man is a good fellow before he has much truck with him—and after all there are worse types. In billets one cannot help noticing him, he is so unlike the others in his indifference to appearances. A big man, heavily built though not very broad shouldered, with clothes a size too large and always looking as if he had slept in them, he is not readily overlooked among these well-turned-out people. He generally wears the baggy breeches the Guards affect, —gents' drop-overs, Mike calls them—puttees that were more frayed than anyone else's, and enormous heavy shooting boots. His coat is like an old Norfolk jacket, and his collar has a way of coming apart from the stud leaving above his shirt a space of white neck that contrasts with his brick red face; for the rest hair rather tousled as if he had repeatedly passed a hand through it, small eyes looking out critically, summing you up and ready to correct exaggeration, a small nose reddened by the sun and a little moustache that he strokes slowly when in thought. Mike and Toby and Jack all call him Uncle, he is really only twenty-eight but nobody looks upon him as anything but middle-aged. He is one of those men who are never really young in the irresponsible young colt fashion. Since we left Armentières he has been coming into his own slowly and almost unnoticed as such people do. You feel you can rely on him, nothing rattles him, he is always the same, sane and level headed, the last man to do anything foolish on the spur of the moment or from impulse. Whatever has happened so far he has remained imperturbable. It seems hardly credible that he had never done a day's soldiering till last August, now he is in command of D company. I feel that he is going to be invaluable if he has the luck to keep on his feet.

In the higher command it is more difficult to appraise the part played by personal virtues in the government of men. The existence of those virtues may not be in question, but it is still necessary to prove that they exercised the power ascribed to them. We who were in France in the First German War did not know that Lloyd George had "won the war" until we returned to England after the Armistice. His optimism, his belief in victory may well have had a considerable effect on the home front, but it is certain that he made little impression on the minds of men in France. Likewise the circumstances in which Haig had to decide to attack in July, 1918, were such that moral courage of a high order was needed. The Cabinet had warned him that they would view heavy casualties with grave concern and that he personally would be held responsible for them. They could hardly have intimated more plainly that in this event he would be removed from his command. No doubt Haig's character did influence those immediately around him. But we in France knew nothing of this man until he was explained to us after the war. Haig with us was not even a legend.

Certainly in France after 1914 there was a tendency for the staff and those in the higher command to lose contact with their troops. There were exceptions of course—Plumer was one of them. In my years with a battalion in the line I penetrated no higher into the military hierarchy than the Divisional General, whom I knew by sight. Once, it is true, when the battalion was in divisional rest after a bad time in the Ypres salient, Haig appeared on the outskirts of the village, surrounded by four horsemen with their turbans and lances to complete the air of make-believe. He enquired of a subaltern where he had been at school and then, as if abashed by his own temerity and without a word to the men, he wheeled about, so that soon he and his little cavalcade were lost in a white cloud of dust.

Yet too much may be made of the gulf between the vast hosts of a modern army and the man who leads. General Wavell has rescued from the Australian Official History an impression of Allenby which I shall borrow here because it brings to life his regeneration of the Egyptian Expedition-

ary Force in the summer of 1917 after their two repulses
at Gaza under Murray in the spring of that year.

There was nothing familiar about Allenby's touch
with his regiments and battalions. He went through
the hot dusty camps of his army like a strong fresh
reviving wind. He would dash up in his car to a Light
Horse Regiment, shake hands with a few officers, inspect hurriedly, but with a sure eye to good and bad
points, the horses of perhaps a single squadron, and be
gone in a few minutes, leaving a great trail of dust
behind him. His tall and massive, but restlessly active
figure, his keen eyes and prominent hooked nose, his
terse and forcible speech, and his imperious bearing
radiated an impression of tremendous resolution, quick
decision, and steely discipline. Within a week of his
arrival Allenby had stamped his personality on the
mind of every trooper of the horse and every infantry-
man of the line.

Men whose personality gives them dominion over others
will not be separated from their followers by any accident
of time and space. In the streets of red Glasgow I have
heard men who had only opened their mouths at politicians
to revile them, murmur "Good Old Winnie"; I have seen
the hard faces of dockers at Rosyth soften when they caught
a glimpse of that formidable jowl, set on the cigar as if he
would crush it, the whole countenance brooding over the
bloody conflict so that his head had sunk into the body
until the neck seemed to have been left out.

But I speak against the rule. I do not suppose personal
magnetism is a potent element in a national army only a
fraction of which can know the Commander-in-Chief by
sight, though I should not dispute its existence in men any
more than I should deny charm in women. Had it more
sway in the smaller armies of the past? There is a picture
of Montrose in chains drawn through the streets of Edin-

burgh to his execution; we see his enemies in tears though they had come to mock at him. We cannot explain how this man, bound and stripped of power, retained his dominion over men. Perhaps if we must speculate on this incalculable personal factor it would be more profitable to take a more recent example, to enquire what was the explanation of Lawrence's hold over his Arabs, or to ask how certain subalterns got their way with their men.

Yesterday Stirling was shot through the head, sniped as he was looking through glasses at the Boche lines. He came to us at Armentières, almost straight from Oxford, a quiet lad of the best type. He was sent to C Company to be under Barty Price. From the beginning the men took to him. When he went out on patrol there was much competition to go with him. He was buried after dark on the edge of the wood. There was no padre—Barty read the service. Spares came over rather frequently and he told us to get down. The men obeyed reluctantly, for they were in no mood to make concessions to the Hun. As Barty found the place there was a rustle of paper that was very distinct in the stillness that had fallen on everything. I looked up involuntarily; everything was so quiet. The moon had risen above the blackness of Zouave Wood in which it was no longer possible to make out the broken shapes of individual trees. The men were half kneeling, their eyes on the ground; Barty who was standing a little apart appeared extraordinarily tall and thin against the sky. He looked up. "You have lost a good officer, men," and then after a moment's silence, "Put him with his head to the enemy." He read the short service, stumbling as he failed to make out the words by the uncertain light of a torch. Then we got up and went away and no one spoke. To-day before we were relieved I walked over to the grave and found that the men of Stirling's company had been working on it overnight. They had marked it out with stones and had planted moss and a few wild flowers that drooped before they took on fresh life.

The art of command is the art of impressing the imagination. Can we take it further?

Yet even in the smaller armies of history I do not doubt that much ascribed to personal magnetism is capable of a more prosaic explanation. The story of the success of Nelson's ship went abroad before men came to swear by his star; Cromwell had first to make his name as a cavalry leader before his personality took possession of his men. General Wavell tells us that when Napoleon asked if a general was "lucky" he meant "Was he bold?" He meant, I think, something quite different. Napoleon had no liking for an unsuccessful general because he knew the part success plays in winning the allegiance of men. Moreover when men have achieved something their spirit bounds up. The secret of success in war is success.

I have divided leadership in an arbitrary fashion into the quality that enables a man to think out what he wants to do and his ability to persuade others to do it. Success is the bridge between; once men are satisfied that their leader has it in him to build for victory they no more question his will but gladly commit their lives to his keeping.

So much needs saying, because those who have attempted to analyse the gift of leadership have often fallen back on an enumeration of all the virtues—there is an early and perhaps rather extreme example of that tendency in Socrates. But soldiers, as I read history, have demanded from their leaders only victories. If they got them they appear to have been content with a mere modicum of personal virtues in their generals. It has been said that character is indispensable for the retention of leadership as well as for its acquisition. If by character is meant a certain integrity of the mind, I can only answer that the facts as far as they are known to me do most obstinately refuse to fit in with that verdict. Some of the great captains—the greatest among them—were supreme egoists. Napoleon maintained the morale of his armies by more than one device, but they had this in common, that each played on the weakness of human nature. He made merry with the aspirations of gullible men. He used men. I could say as much of half a dozen of the captains whose campaigns are the soldier's text book. They had not even the minor graces which make lesser men acceptable to their fellows. They did not see things in perspective—perhaps it is difficult without humour which was denied to nearly all of them—they lived in their plans, centred in themselves so that their troops if they held them in respect had little affection for them, though Marlborough, who was Corporal John to his men, had a place in their hearts.

In the past only victory counted, but if this is the verdict of history it appears to be true no longer. "The first and the last essential of an efficient soldier is character; without it he will not long endure the perils of modern war." I wrote that in 1916 of the battalion officer, it may yet be the crucial test applied to all, high or low, before this conflict ends. For in the great armies of the democracies men who have been torn from the business of peace to fight reluctantly do demand more of their leaders than their forebears; they are no longer content with talent, with the planning gift.

Even in the last war the durability of a General—his survival value—seemed to depend more on character than on capacity. We may doubt the pre-eminence of Foch, Haig, Jellicoe and Trenchard in their art, but as men they came from the old mould of their race, they wore well, they were built for great occasions. In the fundamental clash between great nations, when their existence is at stake, the issue is determined by moral and not by intellectual factors.

I do not mean that the citizen soldier of the modern army, who knows so much more what is going on, will be less insistent on results than the soldier of the past, or that he will make little of the need for brains in his leaders. The attitude of the thoughtful civilian caught up by the last war to the professional army of which he had become an insignificant part was critical. He felt that a man learns soldiering in the same way as he masters any other profession, by the study of the past and by its application to the present. He believed that little could come of such a study unless a scientific mind was brought to bear on the material available. By a scientific mind he meant a passion for exactitude, a craving for proof, and a settled conviction that criticism is essential to healthy thought. He came out of the army in a critical mood, with Loos or the Somme or Passchendaele graven on his mind. His sons, the soldiers of this war, have grown up with those tales in their ears.

As this war dragged into a third winter these soldiers— with their inheritance of doubt—were beginning to wonder whether those in charge of operations in the field did in fact possess this planning gift. If those doubts had been deep and widespread they would have weakened the purpose of the army. Did our leaders possess the ability which wins battles? Were our generals really so inefficient? Those were questions that went echoing down the ranks of the armies of the democracies. We had to find an answer or stand the consequences. The battle of El Alamein gave the answer and the questioning mood has gone. Yet it is still worth while to enquire how soldiers measure the ability of their leaders. No doubt the majority are content to abide by results. But there is a minority who will always question. Will they be given a convincing answer?

For some years now I have come much into contact with soldiers, and I do not subscribe to the humble estimate of their mental equipment that is commonly accepted. Certainly as a doctor I see no reason to believe that a scientific mind is more common in my calling than in the army. At any rate that is true if I am speaking of practising physicians and surgeons. I hasten to add that qualification for there are half a dozen creative minds in the profession of medicine which have no counterpart in the army—Sherrington, Adrian, Dale, Gowland Hopkins, Thomas Lewis, Almroth Wright. There is too no machinery in that service like the Medical Research Council for the discovery of men with the creative instinct at the outset of their careers. Such men would carry out research into tactics and weapons—for example, the limitations of the anti-tank rifle would have been laid down before it was used in battle.

But I am not sure if the conditions of the two professions are strictly comparable. I doubt whether the direction of armies in war calls for the creative instinct in the same measure as does research into the origin of disease. And these doubts are strengthened by a conversation with General Smuts at Cairo in the summer of 1942. I had been talking to him of the appraising, measuring mind, of the value of judgment. He accepted this, but went on to speak of the supremacy of the man of ideas. "Men of action," he said, "live on the surface of things, they do not create." Yet Smuts himself, if he had been born in Germany, might have been one of the great captains of war. He collects his facts like a man of science listening, sifting, rejecting what has not been proved. No other soldier that I know has this approach to evidence. He has been likened to Socrates by the Prime Minister.

Again, I am bound to ask if the conditions of the soldier's life and training are friendly to the development of the scientific mind. Discipline does not foster independence of thought, while life in a regimental mess hardly encourages those habits of reflection that are only bred in solitude. Further there is the fetish, not confined to soldiers, that the mind works best when the body is exhausted by exercise.

I have to ask too if the Army with its code of negatives imposed or enforced in the mess, is tolerant of those individual markings and carriage which often handicap unusual ability. A General must be born to rule men rather than to please them and a strong character should not block the path to promotion. I have had in mind the officers of the regular army. But what must ultimately determine the spirit and purpose of a great host is our success or failure in discovering officers of ability and in promoting them when found. This is the acid test of a democracy at war.

I could put up a barrage of such questions, but I am not certain that the civilian is in a position to criticise the army. The nation gets the army it deserves. I shall be content to support that verdict by a single illustration. Many headmasters of public schools did their best before this war to discourage promising boys from joining the army. They had no doubt good reason for doing so. The subaltern's duties did not fill his day; with the sap running in his veins he woke up to find that soldiering, at any rate at that stage, was not a full time occupation. He was left in charge of a platoon for years, while his contemporaries at school were taking positions of responsibility in other professions. If the lad had been curious and alert the monotony of life with a battalion in peace descended upon him like a damp fog shutting out the light. He was not given an opportunity of mastering one arm after another, he was dumped in an infantry battalion for life.

All this may be true. Yet, be the reason what it may, if we persuade intelligent youth to hold aloof from the Army in peace, we ought not to complain if we are not properly led in war.

We are apt, too, to blame the army for an empirical approach to the art of war that is in keeping with our national character and common to the working life of the country. Our methods are founded on practice and experience; we distrust theory—Foch's books were little read before this war—we are not attracted by mental gymnastics.

The critic of the army should look to the mote in his own eye. Santayana writes: "The truth is the British do not wish to be well led. If they had to live under the shadow of a despotism or a masterful statesman or a deified state, they would not feel free. A certain ineptitude thus comes to be amongst them an aptitude for office. English genius is anti-professional, its affinities are with amateurs." We have been weaned from these fears, but when the war is over they may return.

I have now tried to define how an officer's personality, character, and ability qualify him for leadership. But there is one attribute without which no man can control his fellows—will power. Frederick the Great would not allow his generals to hold Councils of War because they fostered and bred timid courses. Scharnhorst declared that in war it mattered not so much what was done, but that it should be done with vigour and singleness of purpose. In peace a soldier's will is scarcely tested, even self-discipline—the dedication of life to one purpose—is less common than in other professions. So he is put to the final test of war without the necessary self-confidence that he will meet the calls made upon him. Moltke collapsed when in 1914 his plans were not rewarded by immediate success. Falkenhayn restored the situation but lost heart and resorted to half measures after the failure of a flanking attack. Ludendorff could conceive great operations and he was prepared to take some of the risks inseparable from war, but he allowed the possible reactions of the enemy to fill his mind. "He had not," General Hoffmann writes, "the firm will to win victory." When affairs went wrong his nerve gave way. Foch and Haig fortified by their religion were built on stiffer lines. Their will to victory was perhaps their most notable contribution to our cause. The power to drive others to the battle was Foch's gift. A lost battle is a battle that one believes lost. "Mon centre cède, ma droite recule, situation excellente, j'attaque." There we hear the authentic note of leadership. During the second battle in the air in August, 1940, a Minister of the Crown asked where the reserves were. There were none, he was told; the last war plane was in the sky. To send aeroplanes and pilots round the Cape to Egypt at such a juncture was a revelation of will power as impressive as anything in the last war. No other English Government since the last war would have taken such a risk. No other statesman save Churchill, with the possible exception of Arthur Balfour, would have asked it to do so; the decision bore the stamp of a great war Minister.

History may decide that Winston Churchill's first service to the State was that America understood him as she understood no other living Englishman. But when we are gone he will perhaps be remembered as the man who more than any other in the modern world expressed in majestic utterances the unconquerable spirit of a nation. I have been with him more than once when tidings were brought to him of shattering reverses and in my heart I have come to think of him as invincible.

These notes on the virtue of toughness in war would be incomplete without some mention of the President of the U.S.S.R. I have met Stalin twice, but I know nothing of his mind. I see him as he listens to the English case, drawing red wolves on white blotting paper. But what was he thinking about?

Still more is needed: a leader must have the physical resources for the part. A man is as old as his arteries—the old tag is most true in war—and he who makes these calls upon his will power is spendthrift of his days. I have the impression that many senior soldiers and sailors who held high command in the first German war died before their time; they were worn out.

Consider the strain on Haig, first the hazards inseparable from leadership in war; the retreat from Mons and the first battle of Ypres with the very existence of the British Expeditionary Force hanging on a thread. Thereafter came a time of plans gone astray, of immense loss of life; the Somme with its high hopes culminating in sixty thousand casualties on the first day without result; Passchendaele with public disquiet growing; the German break through in March, 1918; and always the little Welshman waiting in Downing Street and watching in open disapproval until the moment was opportune to change his Commander-in-Chief. Yet it has been said that in our army all men of high rank are of an age when both intellectual and physical powers are on the wane. Napoleon when only forty-one years of age, complained that he lacked his former vigour. "The smallest ride is a labour to me." A soldier in a key position lately confessed to me that he could no longer compete with a mass of detail as once he had done.

The strain on mind and body is such that we must do what can be done to lighten the load. If it is necessary to keep a vigilant eye on the fitness of our Generals, it may be as necessary to keep them out of harm's way. It would be of interest to trace how far the exposure of their leaders to repeated bombing contributed to the collapse of the French Army. Few men can trust their judgment when in physical danger. On the other hand men's hearts go to the leader who is ready—as Marlborough and Wellington were—to risk his life. The intrepid General has gone more than half way to win the affections of his men.

When the soldier is at war, his mind should be at peace. I have mentioned the friction between Mr. Lloyd George and Lord Haig. The sharp discords which separated soldiers and politicians in the last war are not to be found in England at the present time. Mr. Lloyd George thought lightly of soldiers, whereas Winston Churchill began life in the army, claims with pride to be a professional soldier, and is versed in military history. It is a matter of importance to him that some detail of drill should be jealousy preserved. He likes soldiers about him, and they feel he is one of themselves.

When I say that the gift of persuading others to do what is wanted is more than half the art of command, I mean by others the "right men". For the art of selection is the secret of leadership. Without this power of devolution staleness seizes upon the harassed leader. In general men given great responsibility work too hard. Gandhi's weekly day of silence for thought and prayer is an example to all Englishmen who hold power. Gandhi found he was "losing mental freshness, spiritual power and was in danger of becoming formal, mechanical and devitalised". The prescription might have been written for any senior Civil Servant. Men of goodwill saddled with the fate of others need great courage to be idle when only rest can clear their fuddled wits.

I have said nothing of religion, though at no time has it been far from my thoughts. General Paget asked me once to talk to officers commanding divisions, and corps, and armies in the Home Forces. When I had done, they broke up and came to me, one or two at a time, questioning. Often that night I was asked about the importance of religion. Speaking as if they did not know how to put it, they separately told me how faith had come into the lives of many of their men. Is it so strange? Boys of this generation have been brought up to believe that war brings the solution of nothing. And yet while still at school they have known that they must pass through an ordeal by battle before they can take up the business of life. Is it not natural that they are fumbling for another way of living, less material, less sterile, than that which has brought them to this pass? What are they seeking?

The story goes that Addison once asked Garth of what religion he was. Garth replied, "Wise men all hold the same religion." "What is that?" said Addison, and Garth answered, "Wise men never tell."